L. & F. Funcken

THE AGE OF CHIVALRY

PART I

Other volumes of The Age of Chivalry

Part 2

Castles, forts and artillery, 8th to 15th century

Armour, 12th to 15th century

Infantry of the Renaissance

Cavalry of the Renaissance

The Slavs and Orientals to the end of the Renaissance

Part 3 – The Renaissance

Arms, horses and tournaments

Helmets and armour

Tactics and artillery

THE AGE OF CHIVALRY

PART 1
The 8th to the 15th century:
Helmets and mail;
Tournaments and heraldic
bearings; Bows and
crossbows

Liliane and Fred Funcken

Prentice-Hall, Inc., Englewood Cliffs, N.J.

Contents

Foreword

In this thirteenth volume of our encyclopedia of military history we take up a fascinating area of study which was barely touched upon in the first volume of *Arms and Uniforms – Ancient Egypt to the 18th Century* published in 1966.

Since that time, our tireless research throughout the museums and archives of Europe, from the humblest to the most prestigious, has enabled us to add a considerable amount to the stock of basic documents on the subject that have been gathered together, despite many obstacles, over a period of twenty-five years.

However it is the early works on the subject that have remained our most valuable guides. The *Dictionary of Architecture* (*Dictionnaire d'architecture*) and the *Dictionary of French Furniture* (*Dictionnaire du mobilier français*) by Eugène-Emmanuel Viollet-le-Duc; *Costume* (*Le Costume*), by Frederic Hottenroth; the *Guide to Arms and Armour* (*Guide des amateurs d'armes et d'armures*) by Auguste Demmin, all of which were written a century ago, are the jewels in the crown of the age which was the first to show interest in the hitherto little-known topic of the medieval period.

It gives us particular pleasure to be able to present to our readers the essence of these authoritative works, which are now practically unobtainable. It gave us even greater pleasure to paint the dozens of figures of every description drawn by these talented pioneers, having rediscovered their sources and followed in their footsteps a century later, all the time realizing with growing admiration just how little their work had dated in that time.

This is only to be expected from works such as these, in which the creative effort that has gone into them is so unmistakable, and so rich, that they evoke in the reader an astonished and enthusiastic response.

The figures drawn in these books, which speak for both the talent of their creators and the vast amount of patience they have unstintingly expended on their work, cast their own fascinating spell. Apart from the phenomenal capacity for work and the insatiable curiosity of these grand old men, they were also excellent draughtsmen, and this gift is a major contributory factor to the appeal their books have for the less scholarly reader.

The material we have borrowed from the above-mentioned authors is confined to the purely military sections of the works; moreover, in borrowing from them we have attempted to add to, rather than simply rewrite, the information they presented originally, and the pages that follow are intended primarily as a tribute to our predecessors. Some of the new theories we put forward in these three volumes are based on our own observations and personal convictions; they do not in any way claim to refute generally accepted ideas, but are intended rather to give the interested reader an opportunity to make a parallel interpretation of the available facts. We await the results of this with the greatest interest.

Our warmest thanks go to our friends Eugène Lelièpvre, artist to the French Army, and Jacques Lesellier, for the valuable information they have passed on to us.

Liliane and Fred Funcken

The sources

The award for seniority among the pioneers must undoubtedly go to an Englishman, Sir Samuel Rush Meyrick, who is considered to be the father of military archaeology. In 1826 he was given the task of reorganizing the famous 'line of kings' in the Tower of London; this was an exciting series of twenty-one equestrian figures at the head of which appeared William the Conqueror – clad in a suit of armour dating from the end of the 16th century! The famous Black Prince who died in 1376 was equipped with a suit of armour that had belonged to Edward VI and had been forged in 1552.

Meyrick, with the enthusiasm of the beginner and the naïvety of the self-taught, rearranged the celebrated row of figures – not, however, without introducing some 'creations' of his own which, although admittedly less bizarre than those that had gone before, were still wildly fanciful. Nevertheless this avid collector awakened the interest of his fellow countrymen in ancient weapons and rusty, ageless old suits of armour.

Forty years later Meyrick's 'scientific method' was held up to ridicule, yet the fact remains that some of the superb pieces on display today in the Wallace Collection (London) come from the gallery of the old pioneer who, even if he was not very scientific, at least had good taste.

Elsewhere the situation was even worse. In Zurich, for example, cuirasses with protruding breastplates were taken for women's armour. In Spain, Italy and Germany – yes, even in scholarly Germany – errors in dating were rife.

In the work by Auguste Demmin mentioned in our foreword, the author vigorously attacked the wrongheaded ideas of museum curators; he was equally critical of France, where a year before a certain P. Lacombe had published [in the charming collection of the Bibliothèque des Merveilles (the

CAROLINGIAN SOLDIERS (i)
1. Carolingian cavalrymen with the imperial standard of Charlemagne. 2. Light infantrymen. 3. Archer. 4. Heavy infantrymen. All the soldiers pictured here are wearing the *byrnie*, a garment resembling the Merovingian *lorica* which in turn had been borrowed from the Romans.

Library of Wonders)] a book called *Arms and Armour*[1] (*Les Armes et les Armures*) in which he had absent-mindedly attributed a suit of armour dating from the beginning of the 17th century[2] to Charles the Bold (who died in 1477).

Demmin's *Guide*, which today is much quoted from and extremely expensive to buy, represented a remarkable step forward for its day, even though some of the interpretations advanced in the book were completely wrong, owing to a combination of a vivid imagination and an excess of reforming zeal – a case of the pot calling the kettle black. However the work remains extremely interesting, and would have constituted a small masterpiece had the author (who was, nevertheless, an excellent draughtsman) taken rather more care over the 1,700 figures with which he illustrated his *Guide*. In contrast, the sixty vignettes chosen by the unfortunate Lacombe are superb examples of his work.

A few years later, in 1874, a truly classic work was published in Paris, *The Descriptive Catalogue of French Furniture (Le dictionnaire raisonné du mobilier français)*, a work in six volumes, was followed the year after by the ten volumes of the *Dictionary of Architecture (Dictionnaire de l'architecture)*; both were lavishly and beautifully illustrated by their author, Eugène-Emmanuel Viollet-le-Duc (1814–1879).

Few authors have been so heavily criticized as Viollet-le-Duc, and today his name is synonymous for most people with restoration that is unwarranted, arbitrary and even bogus. The tourist, his mind poisoned by this slander, looks suspiciously at the castle of Pierrefonds, the town walls of Carcassonne, or the cathedral of Notre-Dame de Paris which the sacrilegious architect stripped without showing any consideration for many of its old statues (these were summarily thrown into the Seine). The tourist need not be alarmed, however, for ten years ago a team of divers from Paris found the 'corpus delicti' (the essential facts of the crime charged).

---

[1] Hachette, Paris, 1868. Demmin was so carried away by indignation that he wrongly takes Lacombe to task for three mistakes too many.

[2] According to Demmin. However, it more probably dates from the second half of the 16th century.

CAROLINGIAN SOLDIERS (ii) and CAPETIAN SOLDIERS

1. and 2. Bodyguard and warrior of Charles the Bald (mid-9th century). They are wearing the iron cuirass called a *thorax* inherited from the Romans; when it was made of leather it was called a *lorica*. The overall effect of the costume is typically Byzantine, and is probably more an indication of the artistic background or origins of the illustrator than an accurate representation of a 'uniform' actually worn in France. 3. Dragon-standard dating from mid-9th century. The dragon continued to be carried into battle until 1270, particularly in Germany. 4. and 5. Capetian warriors of the 10th century. The soldier on the left is wearing a byrnie of metal scales, while the one on the right has on a studded leather byrnie called a trellised byrnie.

ARMOUR IN THE EARLY 11th CENTURY (see page 13)

1. Facsimile of a Norman soldier taken from the Bayeux tapestry (actually an embroidery) which is entitled 'Telle du conquest' – the story of the conquest. The mail-clad trouser-legs are hardly likely to be an accurate representation, given the discomfort they would have caused the rider. (The same opinion has been put forward by our colleague Frederick Wilkinson in his book *Battle Dress*.) In any case the horseman's sword, which he has slid inside his byrnie, would have greatly hindered his leg movements, particularly when he was mounting his horse. 2. Anglo-Saxon knight with a bossed shield. Normans and Saxons also wore byrnies made of round, square or diamond-shaped scales which were riveted or sewn onto a backing of thick cloth or leather. 3. Norman cavalryman dating from the time of the Conquest; he is carrying the standard of William the Conqueror. 4. Traditional presentation of a uniformed Norman soldier according to Hottenroth, Bombled, Large and others. The garment has an exaggeratedly large square yoke which we take to be the opening through which the soldier stepped into these mail breeches. We should perhaps mention that many of the warriors who are pictured in the Bayeux tapestry do not appear to have

THORAX

BYRNIE

TRELLISED BYRNIE

1

2

3

4

5

L. & F. Funcken

People rushed to gaze upon the prized relics that had been saved from vandalism, only to realize they were looking at mere plaster replicas which had been substituted for the statues at the time of the Bourbon Restoration (when the accused was still a child).

The visitor who stands before the impressive bulk of the castle of Pierrefonds would do well to bear in mind the comment of a distinguished archaeologist[1] who wrote, 'In our day (the 19th century) the ruins still appear a remarkably complete unit. Viollet-le-Duc has restored them tastefully and in such a way as to reconstitute overall, if not in detail, an accurate impression of a feudal dwelling of the 15th century'.

Finally, standing beneath the walls of Carcassonne, the tourist can take consolation from the unflattering judgment of Raymond Ritter.[2] The coping of the inner towers, which were restored by Viollet-le-Duc, comes in for a fair amount of criticism; however as the stonework of the towers of the outer curtain wall (built by Philip the Bold) has been preserved, 'Viollet-le-Duc had, therefore, only to restore the floors and the roofing, and so had no opportunity to give free rein to his imagination'.

More often than not the writings of this great pioneer are quoted merely to draw attention to the mistakes in them. This practice is still widespread today, and is especially common among authors of specialist works on Viollet-le-Duc. It is a remarkable fact that whereas a reader looks for what he does not know in a book, the critic seems to be looking only for what the author appears not to know.

If the discredit cast on such a magnificent effort still influences well-informed authors, one can imagine the effect it has on the public at large. Fortunately there are a few military archaeologists whose integrity rises above pettiness of this kind. One such is Philippe Truttmann, who wrote recently, 'Viollet-le-Duc remains the undisputed master in this field of

this supposed opening at the neck. The tapestry also shows the bodies of dead soldiers being stripped of their byrnies; they are being pulled over the head of the victim in exactly the same way as you would take off a shirt – this would, of course, have been impossible had the garment in fact had trouser legs. To take another point, the idea that mail was made up of juxtaposed rings has nowadays been widely discarded in favour of the theory of 'coat of mail' consisting of interlocking rings; all the figures depicted in the famous tapestry would therefore have worn this type of mail, regardless of how it is actually portrayed (see caption to fig. 2). This theory of a standard type of mail has been well and truly discredited by the examples shown on the following page. Experts like the Frenchmen François Buttin and Robert Jean-Charles, who are undisputed authorities on the subject, have never subscribed to over-simplified generalizations of this kind. 5, The square yoke was probably part of the ventail that protected the soldier's face. At the time it was called a 'barb', then later, in the 13th century, it became known as a 'barbel'. The soldier's legs are protected on the outside only. 6. By way of illustrating the theory we put forward in fig. 5, we have shown these two soldiers from Notre Dame du Port (The Church of our Lady of the Harbour) in Clermont-Ferrand, who are wearing the 'barb' in both its raised and lowered position (first half of 12th century).

MAIL (i) (see page 15)
1. French tunic made of twisted leather cording and leather strips, arranged criss-cross fashion (c.1100). 2. Seven different views of garments reinforced with solid mail links. When the mail link was attached by its centre it was said to be 'half-nailed' (de demi-cloure), and when it was fixed by its upper half it was said to be 'top-nailed' (de haute cloure). Both these methods of attaching mail were used until the 14th century. A. 1135. B. 1190. C. 10th–11th century. D. 1110. E. 10th–11th century. By way of contrast this figure (taken from the same manuscript) is shown wearing a 'coat of mail' made of closely-worked ring mail. G. German warrior of the 11th century

---

[1] Camille Enlart, *Manual of French Archaeology* (*Manuel D'archeologie française*), Volume II, p. 614.
[2] *Castles, Keeps and Fortresses* (*Chateaux, Donjons et Place Fortes*) (Larousse, 1953). This work, although short, is packed with information.

HAROLD

1

2

BOSSED SHIELD

3

4

6

5

BARB
BARBEL
VENTAIL

L· A·F·Funcken

study, and his detractors have merely plagiarized his work' (*Archeologia*).[1]

In France the end of the century was marked by the publication of Maurice Maindron's book *Ancient Weapons* (*Armes anciennes*), whilst in Britain Planché and Hewitt produced a classification of the collections in the Tower of London which, though extremely accurate, was improved upon still further by Viscount Dillon, who contributed the results of his thorough study of armourers' marks. Dillon applied the fruits of his research to the new acquisitions made by Sir Richard Wallace, which included several pieces from the collection of the Count of Nieuwekerke, who had been superintendent of the Musée des Beaux-Arts during the Second Empire. These were added to the basic nucleus of Samuel Rush Meyrick's collection to form the renowned Wallace Collection. Although the latter is of less historic interest than the Royal Collection at Windsor Castle, and less impressive than the collection in the Tower of London, it is still one of the finest in Europe.

The largest collection of arms and armour is that of the Kunsthistorisches Museum in Vienna; closely followed by the Armeria Reale in Madrid and the Musée de l'Armée in Paris. Fine pieces are also to be seen in Dijon, Colmar, Brussels, Berne, Basel, Munich, Dresden, Berlin, Turin and Milan.

As far as written documentation is concerned, in 1929 Camille Enlart's famous *Manual of French Archaeology* (*Manuel d'archéologie française*) (parts of which were published posthumously) appeared from out of the wilderness left behind by the First World War. Nothing on this scale had been attempted since the work of Viollet-le-Duc.

Half a century later, in a world which is in an even greater state of turmoil, no new work of this scope has yet been

wearing a tunic of leather or metal scales – hence its name of 'clavaine' or 'clavin' byrnie (from *clavus*, the Latin word for a nail). In the 14th century it was known as a 'clibanion'. 3. 'Plated' mail, which is held in place by thongs or laces. This type of mail, consisting of solid links sewn onto a backing of heavy canvas or leather, has been almost universally interpreted as a fabric of ring mail (the classic coat of mail). It can be seen in many sculptures, and appears flexible and clinging, so much so that it sometimes shows up the outline of the inner and outer malleolus (the projecting bones of the ankle) (see fig. F). In contrast the 'coat of mail', of which there were many accurate representations about this time, hangs quite differently, as can be seen from figs. G. and H. A. End of 13th century. B. 1228. C. 1300. D. 1250. E. 1350. F. 1345. G. 1300. H. 1344.

MAIL (ii) (see page 17)

1. 'Semi-sheathed' (*quasiguesnée*) mail. This rather unusual type of mail has been viewed by most leading writers on the subject as just one more version of the classic 'coat of mail'. Viollet-le-Duc, who became very interested in this mail, gave a highly ingenious explanation of it in which the word 'mail' retained its original meaning of a ring-shaped link; François Buttin, on the other hand, claimed in his book *Du costume militaire au Moyen Age et pendant la Renaissance*, (*Military Costume in Medieval and Renaissance Times*) (1971) that it was made of solid links. The latter distinguished author identifies the particular technique used as being the 'semi-sheathed work' referred to in the statutes of Parisian master armourers of the 14th century. Countless illustrations of this type of mail appear in such manuscripts as the *Histoire du Graal* (*Story of the Holy Grail*) (1280), the *Psautier de Saint Louis* (*Psalter of Saint Louis*) (1252–1270), and the *Grandes Chroniques de France* (*Great Chronicles of France*) (14th century). Other examples have been found engraved in copper on burial plaques, though drawn to a much larger scale; however in our opinion these go to prove that we are not simply dealing with an illuminator's 'dodge' designed to save precious time when drawing detailed repro-

[1] Some art historians have also rehabilitated Viollet-le-Duc. We quote as examples Michel Ragon (*A World History of Modern Architecture and Town Planning* (*Histoire mondiale de l'architecture et de l'urbanisme modernes*), Casterman, 1971–1972): 'This *copyist* is in fact, along with Ruskin, the first major theoretician of modern architecture, and every pioneer in architecture in the 20th century has fully acknowledged this . . . in their early days at least they positively revered Viollet-le-Duc . . . Gaudi in Spain and Guimard in Paris have never tried to conceal their debt to him. . . . We must study the monuments of the past, not in order to copy them, but to work out the principle underlying them. . . . *Any form which we cannot find an explanation for cannot possibly be beautiful*. The theoreticians of functionalism, be they Gropius or Le Corbusier, would not have expressed it any differently'.

1

2

A

B

C

G

D

E

F

CLAYAINE

F. FUNCKEN

3

A

B

C

G

D

E

F

H

published. However, a number of scholarly studies have appeared, in particular those compiled by Charles Buttin during 1906 to 1961, and later by his son François, whose latest work, *Military Costume in Medieval and Renaissance Times* (*Du costume militaire du Moyen Age et pendant la Renaissance*), published in 1971, is a dazzling display of erudition. The articles produced by Robert-Jean Charles, the president of the technical section of the Musée de l'Armée in Paris, have made a significant contribution to the development of a scientific study of medieval arms and armour.

Apart from the many works on the more elaborate or ceremonial type of weapons, books dealing with arms and armour from a general viewpoint are extremely rare. The reader can consult the fine work by Charles Martin called *Arms and Armour from Charlemagne to Louis XIV* (*Armes et armures de Charlemagne à Louis XIV*) (Office du Livre, Fribourg, 1967) which is lavishly illustrated and as easy to read as it is informative; also worth consideration are *Arms and Armour* by Vesey Norman (Weidenfeld and Nicolson, London, 1966), which is more concise, and *Suits of Armour* by Stephen V. Grancsay, curator emeritus of the department of weapons and armour, the Metropolitan Museum of New York, which provides an excellent résumé of the subject in an abridged format. Another Anglo-Saxon, Ewart Oakeshott, has written two magnificent books, *The Archaeology of War* and *The Sword of Chivalry*, which are both standard works of reference. In a series of popularized books for children the same author has published some delightful short works on the subject of the knight and his armour, his horse, his weapons and his castle, as well as on the knight in battle (*A Knight in Battle*, Lutterworth Press, London, 1971); these are masterpieces of scholarly geniality.

Lastly, in German, the weighty tome illustrated by Eduard Wagner, *Costume, equipment and weapons of the late Middle Ages* (1350–1450) (*Tracht, Wehr und Waffen des späten Mittelalters*), published by Artia in Prague in 1960, unfolds for the reader an amazing frieze of costumes, weapons and equipment of all varieties.

ductions of tunics of ring mail. A. Vertical arrangement of links (taken from an illumination). B. Horizontal arrangement of links (large-scale engraving on copper). C. By way of comparison, here is an example of ring mail (large-scale engraving on copper). D. Viollet-le-Duc's interpretation of how the mail was assembled. Front and side views. E. A purely hypothetical simplified version of semi-sheathed mail using solid links; this is included merely to clarify things for the reader. 2. Nailed and laced mail. A great variety of solid links have been found, some of them measuring less than 1cm wide by 2 to 5cms long. It is often difficult to tell how they were attached to their backing. A. Method of top-nailing, as used to make the fauld of a German knight and the aventail of a 15th-century Polish crossbowman. Laced mail is identical in appearance. B. Half-nailed mail (15th century). C. 13th century skull cap. D. Backplate (1395). E. Laced mail (14th century). F. 15th century. G. 14th century. H. 15th century. 3. Jazerant belonging to Jean Zizka, the Hussite leader, who died in 1424. Jazerant mail, which consisted of a varying number of metal plates joined together by interlocking mail, survived in Eastern Europe until the 17th century. It was first worn by the Arabs from the time of the Crusades, if not earlier. 4. Interlocking mail, commonly known as 'coat of mail' today. A. Bascinet with an aventail of interlocking mail and a placcate consisting of nine pieces of plate, dating from the end of the 14th century (1380–90). B. Gorget with sleeves (15th century). C. Gorget in the style of a pelerine, called a 'bishop's cloak' (15th century). D. Arming doublet designed to be worn under a full suit of armour, reinforced with mail to protect the vulnerable areas. E. Simple arrangement of links. F. An open link before being riveted and soldered. G. Zigzag arrangement of links. H. Bronze links bearing the signature of 'Bertolt von Parte' (late 14th century). Readers who would like to know more about the subject of mail in general will find much useful information in the exhaustive study by François Buttin, mentioned opposite.

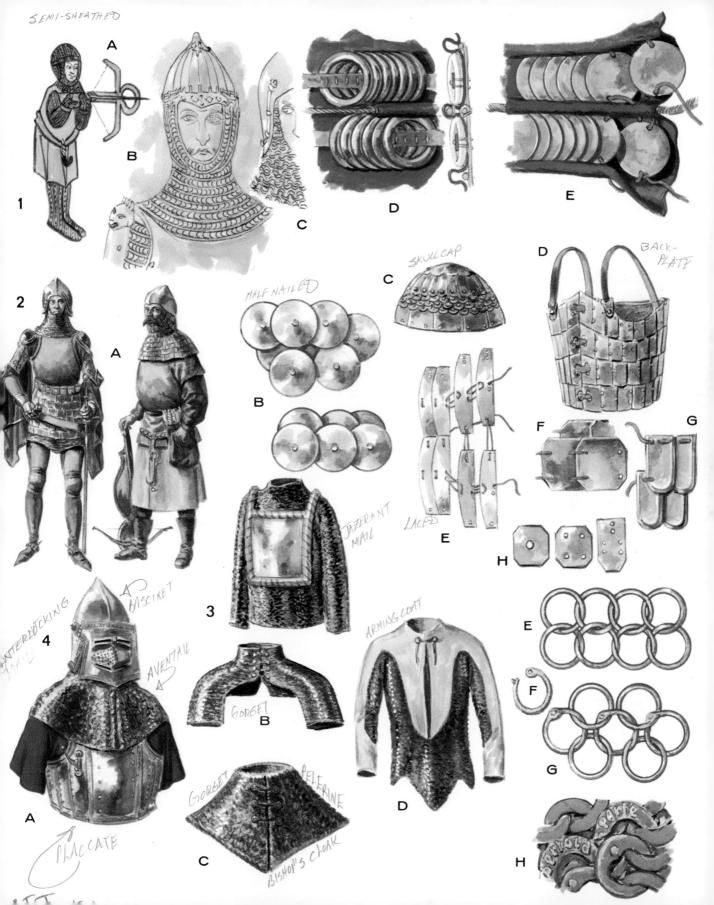

SEMI-SHEATHED

1

A

B

C

D

E

2

A

A

MALF NAILED

B

SKULLCAP

C

D

BACK-PLATE

JAZERANT MAIL

LACED

E

F

G

H

3

4

INTERLOCKING MAIL

BASCINET

AVENTAIL

A

PLACCATE

GORGET

B

ARMING COAT

D

E

F

G

GORGET

PELERINE

C

BISHOP'S CLOAK

H

I HELMETS AND MAIL

In the 5th century AD, the break-up of the Western Roman Empire led to the disappearance of its old military traditions and equipment; these, along with a brilliant civilization, were swallowed up in the wave of Barbarian hordes that swept across Europe.

Generally speaking these Barbarians, whether they were Allans, Salian Franks or Ripuarians, considered it beneath them to wear any form of cuirass.

The decisive victories inflicted on the Visigoths (in 506) and the Saracens (in 732) by the Franks, united under Clovis, and the brave descendants of the Ripuarians who made up the armies of Charles Martel, are proof that the latter were not only well-organized but also possessed a knowledge of the art of war which, though primitive, was nonetheless effective.

Only a very few fragments of equipment have survived from this period of the Dark Ages to the present day.

The Eastern Roman Empire, on the other hand, firmly entrenched behind the vast walls that protected Constantinople from the Bosphorus to the Sea of Marmora, did not suffer the tragic fate of its western counterpart. Icons and miniatures found in manuscripts depict cuirasses made of scale armour, helmets shaped like Phrygian hats, and round or oval shields, all of them appearing strange, contrived and scarcely believable. This picturesque costume appears in Greek manuscripts dating from as late as the 11th century (though with oblong shields in this case), while in Italy military costume of the same period seems to lose its warlike aspect entirely. One exception to this is a type of conical helmet which is sometimes shown with a turban, apparently made of fur, wrapped around it. The miniatures from the Apocalypse of Saint-Sever contain a wealth of examples of these 'amateur soldiers' of the 11th century; we can be certain,

THE HELM AND ITS
DEVELOPMENT (i)
1. German (1100). 2. French (1120). 3. and 4. German (1195). 5. and 6. German (1200). These are also the earliest known examples of crests. They are placed side by side with a pair of wings, a small banner, an eagle's foot and a striped disc. 7. German (1214). 8. English (1214). This may have been the 'new helmet' reportedly worn at the battle of Bouvines. 9. German (1217). 10. French (1230). 11. German (1250). 12. French (1240). 12a. German (1260). Both 12. and 12a. opened sideways. 13. English (1220). This has a ventail that opens upwards. 14. French (1270). This elongated version of the helm lasted only a short time. 15. and 16. English (late 13th century). 17. French (late 13th century). Figs 15, 16 and 17 show helmets fitted with an old-fashioned nasal. 18. French (1295). 19. Crusader knight from the second half of the 13th century. The ailettes on his shoulders, which were made of metal, leather or even stiff parchment, were worn in France from about 1250 to 1325 at the very latest: they became increasingly rare from 1300 onwards.

1

2

3

4

5

6

7

8

9

10

11

12

12 a

13 VENTAIL

14

15

16

17

18

19

AILETTES

L. & F. FUNCKEN.

however, that they have been deliberately denuded of most of their warlike features by the artist himself.

In 9th-century France this 'demilitarized' method of portraying soldiers – even those at the centre of the most terrible massacres – is still to be found in the work of the impassioned, anonymous, illustrator of the school of Rheims and also, up until the 12th century, in the school of Gerona, both of which were influenced by the Byzantine style.

Fortunately rather more convincing élite horsemen and foot-soldiers are portrayed elsewhere; these are shown wearing helmets and cuirasses (of scale armour), or else the Greco-Roman *thorax*. (See for example the illustration of the guards of Charles the Bald, shown in their picturesque 9th-century garb.)

The byrnie

This term, which denotes the oldest military garment mentioned in any French manuscript, appears (in its Latinized form, *brunia*) in the capitularies of Charlemagne, as far back as the year 779.[1]

This garment was originally a sleeveless suit of armour that covered the top half of the body. It was made from a leather or fabric backing, over which were placed round or square links that had been more or less hardened by cementation, i.e. reinforced with steel by a process of heating. These links were arranged in rows, one beside the other, and then fixed to the undergarment by a central rivet. However, the links could also be laid on top of one another, by overlapping them in such a way as to hide the rivets attaching them to the backing. The armour produced by this method had far greater resistance to blows, although heavier and more costly to manufacture.

THE HELM AND ITS DEVELOPMENT (ii)

20. Italian (1280). This famous helmet, called the 'helm of Pavia', was mentioned in 13th century romances. 21. German (1298). 22. and 23. French (late 13th century). The red line indicates the outline of the helmet, which is hidden here by the movable ventail. 24. French (1310). This helm has a crest and was worn in tournaments. 25. German (1318). This helm is fitted with a hat to shield it from the heat of the sun. 26. French (1340). 27. German (1344). It is made of leather and iron, and is fitted with a bevor. 28. French (1370). 29. French (1370). This was known as a 'frog-faced' helm. 30. French (1370). 31. English (1370). 31a. Flemish (1360). Other helmets of the same type as figs. 31 and 31a. have been found in the ruins of the Castle of Tannenberg (destroyed in 1399), and in Denmark and Austria. 32. and 32a. French (1380). Crests were rarely worn in battle, though mitres were sported in battle by warlike bishops in the 13th and 14th centuries. 33. French (1400). At this point the helm stopped developing and eventually disappeared from warriors' equipment around the end of the 15th century; it continued, however, to be worn for jousting until the 16th century. 34. Edward Plantagenet, Prince of Wales, nicknamed the Black Prince, in 1370. As in fig. 35, he is wearing the military belt of a noble, not to be confused with the baldric which was worn in England up until 1420; in France this costly ornament was abandoned twenty years earlier. During his lifetime the famous prince was known by the title of Edward of Woodstock; his curious nickname appeared later, but no-one knows exactly when or why. 35. Charles, Dauphin of France, in 1355. He is wearing a bascinet with a breteche or movable nasal. His helm was worn over a bascinet, as were those in figs. 27, 30, 31 and 34.

---

[1] Capitularies (from the Latin *capitulum*, a chapter) were ordinances set out in chapter form.

IT.

20 1280

GER

21 1298

FR.

22

FR.

23

FR

24 1310

Black Prince

GER

25 1318

FR.

26 1340

27

27 1344

charles Dauphin

BASCINET

BRETECHE

BEVOR

HELM

FR.

28 1370

FROG-FACED

FR.

29 1370

FR.

30 1370

ENG.

31 1370

Flem.

31a 1360

32

32a 1380

33 1400

34

35

L. & F. FUNCKEN

Military service, which was instituted in 802 and levied on a basis of revenue earned from land, was first of all restricted to those who owned three *manses* (a *manse* being the equivalent of 10–15 hectares, depending on the region). This was felt to be too severe, and so the limit was raised to four *manses*; however, according to the capitulary of 813 only the owner or beneficiary of at least twelve *manses* was obliged to present himself for service wearing the byrnie (also known as the *broigne*).

The psalter of Saint-Gall, which dates from the middle of the 9th century and on which our drawing of a dragon-standard is based, shows only two men wearing the byrnie out of a group of nine horsemen. Despite its prohibitive cost, the byrnie was the subject of very strict ordinances limiting the right to wear it; these were issued by Charlemagne, who banned the sale of it outside his borders.

During the 9th century short sleeves were added to the byrnie and it was lengthened to cover the thighs. A matching coif was sometimes added to complete the outfit.

How unrealistic, then, the soldier in *The Dialogues of Saint Gregory* appears a century later; apart from his byrnie of scale armour, he could be the brother of the guards of Charles the Bald we showed earlier wearing the *thorax*. However, it may have been a rough sketch of a particularly elaborately dressed bodyguard.

The byrnie of interlocking mail

Alongside the byrnie made of solid mail there existed a protective garment made of interlaced metal rings. This was a lighter and more flexible garment which was easier to wear but gave far less protection. This was what is known nowadays as the 'coat of mail'; however, the term virtually never appears in texts of the Middle Ages.

This byrnie of interlocking mail seems initially to have been the prerogative of élite men-at-arms, judging by the very precise drawings of the Rodas Bible (10th–11th century); in it only the leaders wear scale byrnies, while the bulk of their mounted troops do not have so much as a breast plate.

MEN-AT-ARMS IN THE 12th and 13th CENTURIES
1. Men-at-arms wearing studded leather (1125). 2. 1150 to 1180. 3. Detailed view of headpieces from around 1180–1200. 4. 1200. 5. 1110. 5a. Detailed view of the strange-looking helmet in fig. 5, which has a fixed nasal, a movable neck-guard and cheek-pieces. Together these protective devices formed the 'clinque'. This unique piece of headgear was discovered by the famous archaeologist Boucher de Perthes. 6. Full-length protective suit of ring mail from the Rhine area (c.1200). The style of garment shown in fig. 2 continued to be worn alongside this trousered model. 7. According to the picture on his royal seal, Richard the Lionheart wore an oblong helmet of Rhenish style (see fig. 6). His descendants preserved his armorial bearings in their original form from 1199 until 1340. 8. Man-at-arms wearing a long surcoat to protect his habergeon from the rain and the heat of the sun (c.1220–1230). The bell-shaped helm is very rare and goes back to around 1200. 9. Man-at-arms wearing a cloth skull-cap shaped like a turban: also called a 'mortar' (1220–1230). 10. From 1250 onwards the surcoat tended to get shorter, though there are many examples of long surcoats continuing to be worn until the mid-14th century. The true date of these coats is indicated by details of the accompanying armoured defences. The garment all these 'ironclad' men are wearing is nowadays called a hauberk, but in Latin countries it was known as a 'jazerant' up to the end of the 13th century. The byrnie of solid mail was for a long time the basic equipment of the less well-off soldier, and even when the costly 'coat of mail' was worn it did not always cover the legs, for reasons of economy. Yet were all these garments really made out of ring mail, as is now widely claimed? Most artists of the period used a simplified method to represent the universal 'coat of mail', but one of them, the illustrator of a medical treatise preserved at Ratisbon, has reproduced several types of mail in great detail, including ring mail, solid round mail arranged in horizontal rows, studded leather and oblong mail in the form of scales

1

1125

2

1150-80

3

5a

CLINQUÉ

MORTAR

4

5

8

9

6

7

10

L. & F. FONCKEN

Mail

The Bayeux Tapestry

This famous piece of embroidery, which is over 74 metres long, is said to have been made by Queen Mathilda, and is of special interest to the student of military equipment in the 11th century.

This gigantic 'comic strip', embroidered on linen cloth in eight different shades of woollen thread, depicts with a surprising verve and eye for detail the events of the conquest of England by William of Normandy. Although it has often been described as crude and primitive in execution, its elongated figures and stereotyped gestures irresistibly call to mind a child's drawing. It is interesting to note that the embroiderers, who were probably working from a cartoon or preliminary sketch, altered the original drawing somewhat and even reversed the chronological order of certain scenes.

The sketchy, vague drawings of the mail of the byrnies worn by combatants on both sides have given rise to countless studies and an equal number of arguments. The highly respected Sir Samuel Meyrick thought he could make out eight types of chain mail garment. This was reduced to the more reasonable figure of three by Meyrick's successors, Demmin, Viollet-le-Duc, and Hewitt. They settled for the three following types of mail:—

1. ringed mail made of links placed one next to the other;
2. mail made of oval-shaped links, each one half-covered by the following link;
3. mail made of diamond-shaped links, each one overlapping the other like tiles on a roof.

In 1931 the Englishman F. M. Kelly dismissed this terminology in peremptory fashion, claiming that it was pure invention. In his opinion mail should be described in one way and one way only, namely as a metal ring which, when

THE BASCINET (i)
1. Small bascinet with a mail breteche. 2. Small bascinet with a breteche (1370). 3. Small bascinet with a breteche and a pivoting closure shaped like a fleur-de-lys (1370). 4. Bascinet with a long proboscis-shaped visor (1300). 5. Bascinet with a bulbous visor (1310). 6. Bascinet with a visor and bevor (1350). 7. Italian bascinet with a visor (1360). 8. English bascinet with a visor (1360). 9. Gunther de Scharzburg, who died in 1360. He is wearing a bascinet with a movable breteche. His armour is made of leather reinforced with gilded metal.

24

1

BRETECHE

2

3

4

5

6

VISOR

BEVOR

7

8

9

L. & F. Funcken

interlaced with others, formed a single coat of mail. This theory of Kelly's, which many people subscribed to, still has its supporters, although the leading experts of today reject this interpretation as being too simplistic.

Simply studying documents of the period, some examples of which we have reproduced here, in our view provides conclusive evidence as to the true composition of mail; however we cannot recommend too highly to the more exacting of our readers the scholarly work on the subject by François Buttin, based on research into texts of the period.

The byrnie of solid mail and the coat of ringed mail existed side by side until the former gradually began to lose ground and finally disappeared from use altogether in the early years of the 14th century.

Interlocking mail

The cuirass made of interlocking mail was known to the Romans, who credited its invention to the Gauls. They called it *lorica hamata* or *lorica conserta hamis*, from *hamus*, the name for the metal ring used. Less than a century before the birth of Christ Varon of Narbonne defined it even more precisely as a tunic made of iron rings, *ex annellis ferrea*. The difficult technique of making this mail was forgotten after the devastation of the Barbarian invasions, and had almost completely died out. The rarity of the garment meant it was reserved for the better-off.

The claim has sometimes been put forward that the first garments of circular mail were brought back from the East by the crusaders, but this is patently false. The only knowledge Princess Anna Comnena, who was usually so inquisitive about the things of her age, had of this new mail fabric was from having seen it worn by knights from the North, which is ample proof of its comparative rarity in the 12th century. However, it is not unreasonable to suppose that when the crusaders came up against the Infidels, who were equipped with light and, above all, well-ventilated suits of armour (vitally important in the burning heat of the East), they were quick to adopt a

THE BASCINET (ii)
1. German bascinet with its visor suspended in the same way as a breteche; this type of visor was known as a *Klappvizier* (1350). 2. and 3. German bascinets with suspended visors (1370 to 1380). 4. English bascinet of the same type as the previous models with its 'snap-visor' (1370). 5. Italian bascinet (1390). The 'hounskull' is made with no ventilation holes on its left side so as not to weaken the helmet's resistance to lance thrusts (see figs. 1 and 7). 6. Italian bascinet (1380). 7. Italian bascinet (c.1400). 8. French great bascinet with a colletin. 9. French great bascinet with a gorget-cum-colletin (1400). 10. Italian great bascinet *alla francese* (1445). The great bascinet was worn throughout Italy and Western Europe until around 1420–1430; in Germany, however, it remained in use a little longer, until 1440. 11. Bertrand du Guesclin (c.1380). The indomitable little Breton, who was dubbed 'more of a cowherd than the son of a knight', began his military career at the age of eighteen. Here he is armed with the great sword for use in foot combat. This sword, which was too long to be worn at the side, hung from the pommel of the knight's saddle. It is a modified version of the old 'brand', which was called the Viennese or Pavian brand and was much favoured by knights in the second half of the 13th century. It is the original 'brand of light steel' or 'brand hanging from the pommel' referred to in the *chansons de geste*. We have based our drawing of Du Guesclin's face on the effigy on his tomb at Saint-Denis. Rarely has such an ugly countenance concealed such a chivalrous soul.

1 BILLARD VIZIER

5 PITOUNSKOLL

GORGET-CUM-COLLETIN

COLLETIN

L. & F. FUNCKEN

similar kind of protective garment. Moreover they did so all the more readily because the enemy's fighting methods were admirably suited to this type of garment; the typical pattern of the massed charge with the heavy lance, followed by hand-to-hand fighting with the equally heavy sword of the Franks, was quite unknown to them.

Our ancestors were fully aware of the vulnerability of interlocking mail and it was only used extensively after it had been covered with steel 'plaques',[1] or at the very least with metal that had been surface-hardened by successive firing and chilling. These plaques, designed to cover the trunk and the limbs, became more and more close-fitting until eventually they looked like gutters that totally enclosed the limbs; this in turn gave rise to the full suit of armour, the so-called 'white harness'.

The progress brought about in the manufacture of mail thanks to the invention of wire-drawing in the 13th century, as well as the improvements made to it by craftsmen like Rudolf the German, popularized the coat of mail and placed it within the reach of the humblest fighting man. In addition it had the tremendous advantage of being easily repaired and, above all, easily adjusted to fit different measurements: all that had to be done was simply to add or take away the required number of links. Mail nevertheless gave no protection against the severe blows inflicted by steel weapons or against arrows fired by the longbow; this holds true to an even greater extent for the formidable bolt of the crossbow.

This brings us on to François Buttin's remarkable study, which topples all previously held theories, on the correct meaning of the word 'mail'. The sheer weight of argument, backed up by close textual analysis, compels our attention.[2]

Is it in fact conceivable that people were prepared to abandon the impervious byrnie for the slight protection of

THE BARBUTE

The barbute, which originally came from Italy, was eventually worn all over Europe, though usually with the addition of a bevor, or, more often, a mail aventail. In the latter form it can be mistaken for a small bascinet without a visor. In Germany the barbute was known as the 'Italian sallet'. Again, there are some experts who call this type of helmet a sallet, while others classify it in the same category as the barbute. Speaking for ourselves, we have chosen to reserve the term 'sallet' for those models which have no cheekpieces and whose neck-guard is conspicuously long, and which thus point to the classic sallet with its distinctive features. 1. Italian (1370). 2. Italian (1450), 3. Italian (1460). 4. Barbute with a nasal and visor that bears a strong resemblance to the bascinet (c.1400). 5. Italian (1460). 6. Italian (1470). 7. Italian crossbowman (1370), wearing a barbute influenced by the helmets of the hoplites of ancient Greece and a jack made of thick fabric that serves as body armour. The small nasal of the Italian barbutes did not survive later than 1450. 8. Infantryman wearing a barbute which has roundels, a hinged bevor and a gorget (c.1450).

---

[1] 'Plaques' are often confused with 'plates', which were used only to reinforce a leather or fabric garment designed to protect the upper half of the body: this was the 'plate coat', or 'steel coat'. The term 'plate armour', which is often used for the 'white harness', is quite incorrect here.

[2] *Military Costume in Medieval and Renaissance Times*, Real Academia de Buenas Lettras, Barcelona, 1971.

cheek pieces that cover most of the face

1

2

3

4

5

6

7

8

L. & F. FUNCKEN

mail coats and shirts, which, although admittedly lighter, were so very vulnerable without additional reinforcing plaques? Would the warriors of the 11th, 12th and 13th centuries have shown such a disregard for the most elementary safety, simply for the sake of being a little more comfortable? The study of military costume in the Middle Ages testifies rather to an unceasing quest for a means of ensuring complete protection for even the smallest area of the body – a quest, moreover, which it is hard to reconcile with the notion of heroism inherent in the age of chivalry.

Solid mail

The scale armour of the early byrnies was replaced by solid mail, which, as François Buttin has demonstrated, was held together by nails or laces. This now became the basic material used in making those garments which were shaped to fit the arms and legs closely and which have been confused with what we nowadays call 'coat of mail'.

THE KETTLE HAT (i)
1. German military hat (12th century). 2. Bohemian military hat (13th century). 3. Skullcap-cum-kettle hat (early 13th century). 4. Kettle hat (1350). 5. Kettle hat modified to fit over a barbute with a bevor (1350). 6. Kettle hat (14th century). 7. English man-at-arms (c.1330). The weapon he is carrying is a bardiche. 8. German footsoldier (c.1380). He is wearing a kettle hat with a nasal and a gambeson padded with tow.

1

2

KETTLEHAT

3

BARBUTE

BEVOR

5

4

BARDICHE

GAMBESON

6

7

8

The helmet

The safety precautions prompted by the most basic instinct for survival were chiefly directed towards protecting the head, the part of the body that was most fragile and exposed to blows.

The helm

The word 'helm', from the German *Helm*, was the name already used to describe the military headpiece of Carolingian warriors, which was rather similar in appearance to the morion. This was superseded by a conical helmet with a fixed nasal, or nose-piece, and sometimes an additional neck-guard. It was described as 'Norman' in shape, and was, in fact, probably introduced by the Normans or Scandinavians. It was soon followed by a model with a domed crown, the *Kalottenhelm*, which originally came from North Germany.

The helm proper, as described in present-day terminology (i.e. a kind of box covering the entire head), was more accurately termed *Topfhelm* (from *Topf*, a pot) in German; later the term *Kugelhelm* (from *Kugel*, meaning a ball or globe) was used to describe the high-crowned helm dating from the beginning of the 14th century.

The helm, or at any rate the first primitive version of it, appears in the work by the Abbess Herrade de Landsberg,[1] the *Hortus deliciarum* (*The Garden of Delights*), in the form of a perforated ventail riveted on to a conical helmet. A similar arrangement was adapted for use on German helmets with a domed crown. This ventail grew rapidly in size from the end of the 12th century onwards, until a few decades later it ended up as the classic helm with which we are familiar.

The crown, which was originally flat, proved too vulnerable

---

[1] One of the oldest known encyclopedias, written around 1190 at the Abbey of Mont-Saint-Odile, in the diocese of Strasbourg.

THE KETTLE HAT (ii)
1. Kettle hat with a bevor (1420). 2. Montauban kettle hat. At the beginning of the 15th century the kettle-hat visor first appeared in France in this southern town – hence the name. The visor had two vision-slits pierced in it. 3. Kettle hat with a riveted brim (1450). 4. Kettle hat (1460). A. The regular brim of these helmets is the sole feature that distinguishes them from the sallet. 5. Footsoldier wearing an unusually-shaped kettle hat and a sleeved brigandine reinforced with steel strips and a metal aventail (*c*.1400). 6. Soldier belonging to the citizen's militia of Paris during the reign of John the Good (*c*.1360). The troops of large European towns readily displayed the colours of the town coat of arms, which they often painted on their helmets. 7. Footsoldier wearing a kettle hat and brigandine with vertical slashes (1440). The example here shows the kettle hat in the final stages of its development. The kettle hat was very common all over Europe in the Middle Ages. In particular it gave the infantryman excellent protection against blows dealt from above by mounted troops.

1

BEVOR

2

3

A

4

5

6

7

— & F. Funcken

to the blows dealt by the heavy weapons that had been admitted into the range of standard equipment and represent the degeneration of the old spirit of chivalry in the two previous centuries. The crown became increasingly conical in shape so as to ward off blows from above. It is interesting to note that the helm seems to have been worn comparatively rarely in Spain, where it was replaced by a kind of bowl-shaped skull cap.

These two types of helmet were literally daubed with the heraldic colours of their owners.

The conical helm, which was originally worn over a kind of padded cowl, a mortar or a skullcap made of hide or metal, grew in height and was eventually worn over a small helmet. This in turn rested on a hauberk, a kind of hood covering the head and shoulders and reaching to the chest.[1] During the 14th century the hauberk gave way to the aventail, which was attached to the stapled bascinet by means of silk laces; it had, however, no coif.

The bascinet

From being used initially as a supplement to the helm, the bascinet gradually evolved along separate lines into a piece of protective armour in its own right with the addition of suspended or pivoting visors of varying shape. In the final stage of its development, towards the end of the 14th century, it acquired the snout-shaped faceguard known as a 'hounskull' visor; particularly fine examples of this were made by Italian armourers around 1390–1400.

The final improvement to the bascinet consisted of reinforcing the inadequate protection which the aventail offered the throat by covering the area with an iron gorget. Thus the great bascinet was born.[2]

THE SALLET (i)
1. Barbute-sallet (1350). The rivets were for holding the inside lining of the helmet in place. 2. Footsoldier's sallet without a visor (first half of the 15th century). This helmet, like the following ones, was fitted with a strap that fastened under the chin. 3. Cavalryman's sallet with a 'restricted sight' (first half of 15th century). 4. Footsoldier's sallet with a fixed visor (second half of 15th century). 5. Sallet with a fixed set-in visor. This was a French type of sallet that was comparatively easy to forge (mid 15th century). 6. Knight's sallet with a movable visor (1440). The spring-mounted push button (a) kept the visor lowered. 7. Sallet with a movable visor and laminated neckguard, lowered and ready for combat (1460). 8. As above, when it was not being used in combat. 9. French sallet with a movable visor (1450). 10. Cavalryman wearing a sallet and suit of armour typifying the transitional stage between so-called plate armour and iron armour (1400). The compact version of the sallet was called a sallet 'in the French style', while the version with a long neck-guard was known as a sallet 'in the German style'.

---

[1] See *The Hauberk* see part 2 of *The Age of Chivalry*.

[2] The 'great bascinet' is often called the 'hounskull' bascinet; the term 'small bascinet' is reserved for the type without a visor. We use the term 'great bascinet' to describe the bascinet with gorget, which in our view is the only one that deserves this name.

1

2

3

4

5 FRENCH STYLE

a

6

7 GERMAN STYLE

9

10

8

L. & F. FUNCKEN

The armet

This term is a corruption of the Old French 'hiaumet' and the English 'helmet'. The armet, a type of small helm, was the natural successor to the bascinet and finally reached that stage of perfection which was to make it the last, completely unrivalled military headpiece of the Middle Ages.

The armet was instantly recognizable on account of its rounded shape, 'close to the head', which silhouetted the chin and neck of the wearer. A later hybrid version of the sallet, which we have christened the 'sallet-armet', did not have this complete protection for the neck and required separate pieces to be added as reinforcements.

The sallet

The classic sallet is German in origin; its name comes from the German *Schale*, meaning 'cup' (hence *Schallern*, *Schelern* and, in modern times, *Schaller*).

In translating the Italian word *celata* by 'sallet' Demmin (op. cit. page 281, fig. 72) provoked a misunderstanding which persists to this day. Previously people had based their interpretation of the word on the Latin *caelata cassis*, meaning 'chiselled helmet' (a patently absurd idea), while the verb *celo*, meaning 'hide', gave *celatus*, which is a far more acceptable etymology. The special feature of the *celata veneziana* was that it concealed most of the face underneath a small nose-piece and wide 'cheeks'; however it bore no similarity to the classic sallet. For this reason we have grouped the Italian *celata* with the barbute, its twin sister.[1]

The early sallet was very similar in appearance to the most basic shape of helmet, which left most of the face uncovered and was worn by the humble foot-soldier; the sallet, however, could be distinguished by its elongated neck-guard. It would probably be an exaggeration to give the name of 'sallet' to this first tentative version, which we call the 'barbute-salet'.

[1] In the Tower of London the term *barbuta* is used to mean the *celata*.

THE SALLET (ii)
1. Infantryman's sallet with a bevor (1440). The bevor was always attached to the breastplate of the cuirass, never incorporated with the sallet. 2. Infantryman's sallet (1450). 3. Infantryman's sallet (1450). 4. Sallet with a movable visor and a non-laminated neck-guard (1460). 5. Sallet with a movable visor (1480). Note that in figs. 4–6 the opening for the sight is not in the visor itself. 6. Sallet with a movable visor and bevor (1480). 7. Elegant sallet with a fixed visor, made in Bologna (1490). In Italy the movable visor was said to be *alla tedesca* – 'in the German style'. 8. Sallet in the final stages of its development (late 15th century). By this time it is virtually identical to the armet. The movable visor shown here was called a 'bellows' visor. 9. Full suit of Italian armour weighing 25 kilos (1435). 10. Armour worn by Jean Poton de Xaintrailles, companion to Joan of Arc (*c*.1435). In this case the helmet is not a sallet but a kettle hat with a bevor. The sallet, which replaced, and greatly improved upon, the bascinet, was worn alongside the armet until the 16th century.

1

2

3

4

SALLET

KETTLE HAT

5

7

6

9

10

8

BELLOWS VISOR

L. & F. FUNCKEN

Once the sallet had acquired its final shape, it enjoyed enormous popularity. Although it was much less comfortable to wear than its rival, the armet, it held out for a long time against its competitor, even though towards the end it strove to imitate it. This model is what we earlier dubbed the 'sallet-armet', and its defects are clearly shown up by the illustrations.

The barbute

The *barbuta*, which is typically Italian in style, is known as an 'Italian sallet' in Germany and a 'French sallet' in France. When a visor is added, it becomes either a 'bascinet with faceguard', a 'barbute with visor', or a 'barbute with staples'.[1] This remarkable degree of confusion is evidently due to the similarity in shape that exists between the bascinet and the barbute, if we ignore the peculiar feature of the latter, namely the 'cheeks' that almost entirely cover the sides of the face. For the purpose of this work we have made this characteristic feature the basis for drawing what we believe to be a necessary distinction between the two types of helmet.

The kettle-hat

This type of armoured hat first appeared in the 13th century, and its design was initially a rather timid borrowing from civilian fashion. It soon developed a wide brim, so that when viewed from above it looked rather like a round shield. Indeed the special model worn by sappers, which had an extra-wide brim, was actually used like a shield.

In the next stage of the evolution of the kettle-hat the brim was lowered, after undergoing various short-lived modifications which were directly related to developments taking places in weaponry. Hence the model ended up as something closely resembling the sallet before reverting to its original

THE ARMET (i)
1. Bycocket or bycoket, often mistaken for the great bascinet (shown in fig. 2). It was worn only rarely in France (*c.*1450). It opened up into two halves, rather like an Easter egg. The visor opened from the side. 2. Great bascinet in the final, perfected stage of its evolution (1400). The example here marks the transitional stage between the bascinet and the armet. 3. *Idem* (1410). 4. German bycocket (1440). In fact this helmet is already an armet in all but name, and it has the latter's characteristic parts and hinges. 5. Italian armet with vervelles or staples (1430–40). The visor has been reconstructed. This model already incorporates all the characteristic features of the true armet. 6. Armet with a concealed visor-hinge and reinforced front; made in Milan (1450). 7. Italian armet (1451). 8. Armet of which only one copy was made (1430). The jagged edge considerably reduced the dangerous width of the *vidaille* (the slit was left to look through when the visor was lowered). Here the visor, which is missing, has been reconstructed and its outline drawn in in red. 9. The same armet opened up (front and back views). The mark of the master armourer, a capital T, can just be made out (this letter has sometimes been wrongly attributed to Tomasso dei Negroni). The staples, incidentally, served to hold in place the colletin of ring mail that was meant to protect the join of the helmet and the cuirass. The helmets in figs. 4, 5, 6 and 8, which were shaped to fit into the neck, all opened as shown in fig. 9.

[1] In the splendid workbook by the late lamented Maurice Leloir, *The dictionary of costume* (*Dictionnaire du Costume*, Gründ, Paris, 1951), examples are given of a barbute which is described as 'simple' but which is both stapled and breteched; two barbutes which are called 'sallets'; and a sallet which is in fact a helm (pages 29, 75, 372).

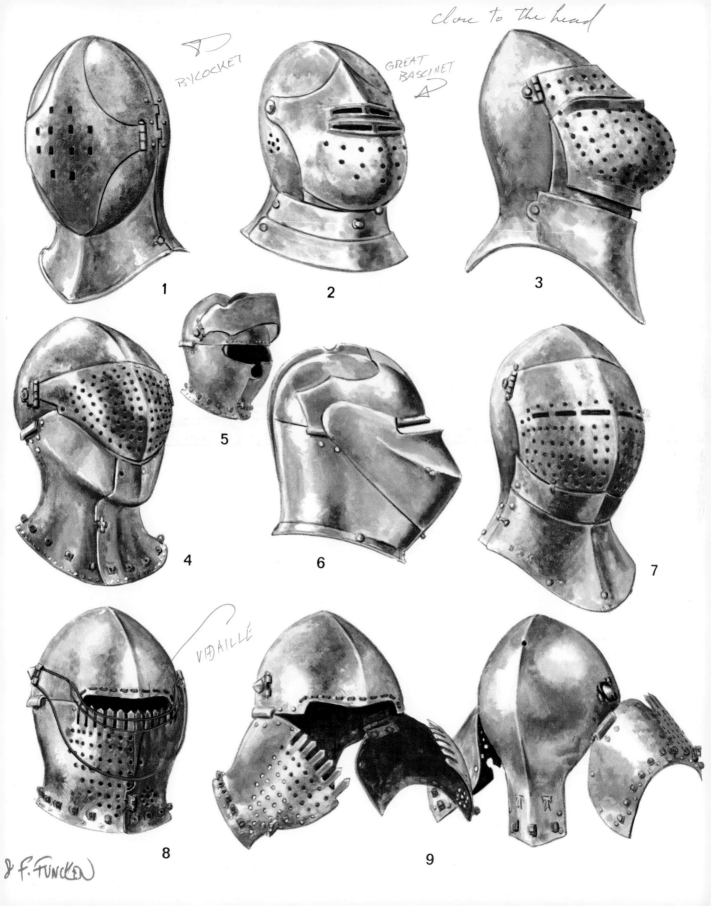

BYCOCKET

close to the head

GREAT BASCINET

VIDAILLÉ

1

2

3

4

5

6

7

8

9

J. F. Funcken

shape with the horizontal brim around the mid-fifteenth century. This final shape was to give rise to the morion, the cabasset, and eventually a hybrid version known as the 'morion-cabasset'.[1]

THE ARMET (ii)

1. Full suit of German armour dating from the middle of the 15th century; its armet extends to cover the throat, and the gorget also pivots open. This suit of armour is a masterpiece of skilful design and manufacture, and weighs only 25 kilos. Armour was strictly 'made to measure', and was designed to fit the shape of the wearer's body. Notice here the curve of the vastus lateralis muscle (a), the vastus medialis (b), the sartorius (c), the hamstrings (d) and (e), the peroneus longus (f), and the soleus (g). The result of the individual design is the lifelike appearance, the natural proportions and posture which Stephen Grancsay of the Metropolitan Museum of New York has described so well in his book *Suits of Armour*; it was this that made these 'hollow statues' so difficult to forge. 2. The armet of fig. 1 viewed in profile. The upper part with its vision slit was called the sight, while the lower part was called the ventail; together these two pieces formed the *mézail*, or faceguard. This was adopted from the late 15th to 16th century, but the old *vidaille* (see figs. 5 and 6), which did not incorporate a vision slit, was not entirely supplanted until 1520. 3. Back view of the armet in fig. 1. The two hooks are the rests for the spaudlers. The helmet was donned by opening up the bevor. Once the pin (a) was removed, the advantage of this method over the old one was that the chin defence was in one piece rather than two (for an illustration of the old method see figs. 5 and 6, and also figs. 4, 5, 6 and 8 on the previous page). 4. Armet with its visor raised and its bevor open. The visor is made in one piece, and the bevor pivots on a single hinge, as in figs. 1, 2 and 3 (1470). 5. Florentine armet with a reinforced front dating from about 1490; this was the period when armour decorated with engraving and damascening first began to appear. 6. and 7. Armet (late 15th century). The rondel (a) was meant to conceal and protect the place where the cheek-pieces of the movable ventail met. The tail or stem (b) held an inside strap that attached the armet to the backplate. These helmets each weighed between 3 and 4 kilos, but the versions used in jousting, although identical in appearance, weighed over 5 kilos apiece.

[1] See Part 3 of *The Age of Chivalry*.

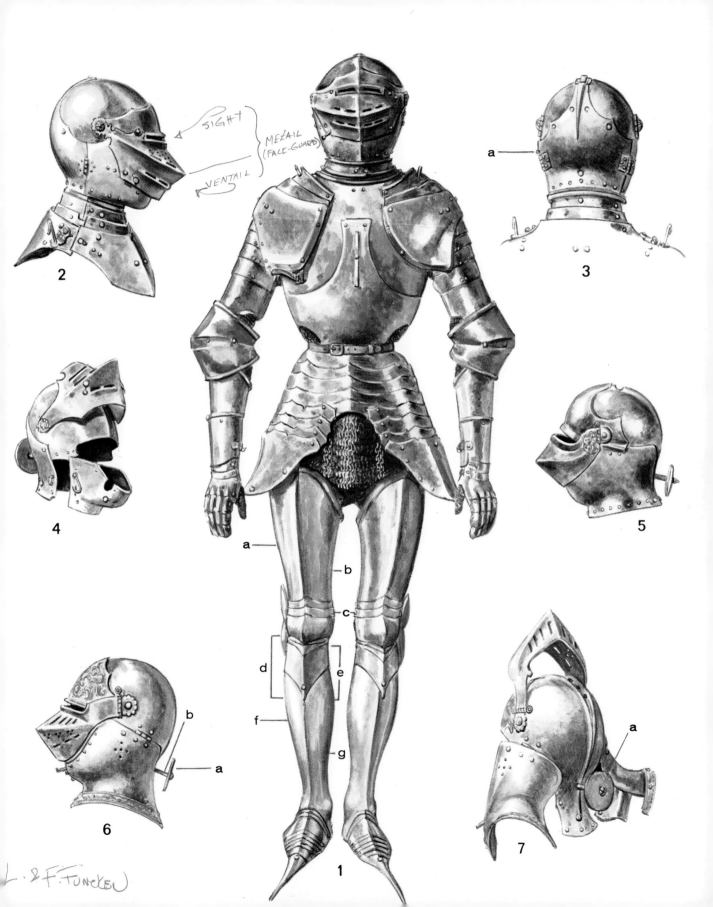

SIGHT

MEZAIL
(FACE-GUARD)

VENTAIL

2

3

a

4

5

6

b

a

7

a

a

1

b

c

d

e

f

g

L. & F. Funcken

II TOURNAMENTS AND HERALDIC BEARINGS

Charlemagne, together with his peers and paladins (officers of the royal household), had already replaced the old infantry with a heavily armed cavalry as early as the 8th century. This great emperor had already attached an élite body of warriors to his person by granting them 'benefices' in the form of land concessions which were held in return for fulfilling the *auxilium*, or military service.

The fratricidal strife among Charlemagne's grandsons, the Viking invasions and the anarchy they caused, committed the *senior*, or seignior, to securing the support of as many *vassi* (vassals) as possible.

Henceforth the social structure was simply a hierarchy based on the amount of land owned by warriors who, as they were all subordinate to one another, formed a chain of command that went from the enfeoffed knight (i.e. one who had been granted land, or a 'fief') up to the king himself, whose direct power was now confined to the area of his own domain. The enfeoffed knight owed obedience to his suzerain alone; he was only subject to the king's authority via the intermediary of his own lord and protector. This is what we call the feudal system.

CRUSADER KNIGHTS
1. German knight (late 12th century). 2. French knight (late 12th century and very early 13th century). 3. Italian knight (late 12th century). The helm, which is shown here in its most basic form, could also be conical or domed, with or without a nasal. 4. Flemish knight (first half of 13th century). 5. English knight (second half of 13th century). Like the knight in the previous figure, he is wearing a turban-style skullcap (sometimes called a mortar) which formed a layer of padding that helped to keep the helm upright without hurting the forehead and temples of the wearer. 6. French knight (*c.*1270). It was only after the end of the first two Crusades, from 1189 onwards, that the emblem of the red cross was abandoned by all except the French crusaders. The English chose to wear a white cross instead, while the Germans adopted a black cross, the Italians a yellow cross and the Belgians a green cross. This decision is a striking illustration of the lack of unity between those countries taking part in the Crusades at the time; it also shows the extent to which the ideals of the early Crusaders had declined.

The knightly orders

Knighthood proper, that is the sacramental order glorified in medieval *chansons de geste*, or verse-chronicles, should not be confused with the feudal status of the enfeoffed knight.

This new, independent knighthood, called the knightly

orders, was not formed until the 11th century. Its object was to embody the ideals of justice, law and order during what were particularly troubled times in a society completely dominated by the violence, coarseness, cruelty and unscrupulousness of the feudal era.

The Church did all it could to make war more humane. The 'peace of God' of 969 gave protection to civilians and their possessions, while the 'truce of God' of 1027 forbade fighting to take place on Sundays; in 1041 this period of truce was extended from Wednesday evenings to Monday mornings. It was against this background that the ambitious project of uniting the warrior and the Christian in one ideal being was formed. The idea was Utopian, admittedly, yet it created a way of life that was far from being sterile. The Church, in giving its blessing to the expeditions that set out to fight the Infidels, was providing a safety-valve for men who had need of action, who were tough and passionate and susceptible to mystical ideas.

The knight, whose adherence to an order was sanctified in a series of moving ceremonies,[1] became the legendary hero who is for ever present in our memories.

This was the élite body to which the knights errant of the 11th and 12th centuries belonged. These 'illustrious fools' roamed Europe, solitary travellers who lived on raw venison pressed between two stones, the traditional 'food of heroes'. It was said that they had only to sound their horn outside the gates of a castle to obtain food and lodging; however, this method cannot always have been successful, since some texts state that castellans offering hospitality took care to place a helm at the top of their keep as a sign of welcome.

As an independent body the knightly order had its own hierarchy, and formed a military brotherhood that brought considerable benefit to its members. Then it foundered in anarchy and disappeared, making way for purely military orders like the Knights of the Sepulchre, the Knights of Saint John of Jerusalem, the Knights of Saint Lazarus, the Knights

KNIGHTLY ORDERS
1. Knight of the 'Compagnia della buona morte' in 1176. Although there is no comparison between this brotherhood, which illustrates the bombastic Italian approach, and the other orders shown here, it did nevertheless distinguish itself under the command of Alberto da Guissano against the Imperial forces. 2. Banner of the kingdom of Jerusalem in the 13th century. 3. Knight Templar in the 13th century with the standard of the Order of the Temple, known as 'Beaucéant'. The black of the flag symbolized strength and the white purity. 4. Knights of the Sacred Sepulchre in the 13th century. This religious and military body was similar to the Templars. Its members withdrew to Italy after the fall of Palestine. 5. Knight of the Order of the Sword-Bearers, known also as the Order of Livonia. In 1237 this Order amalgamated with that of the Teutonic knights, thereby substantially reinforcing it. 6. Teutonic knight of the 13th century. 7. Teutonic knight carrying the standard of the Order. This emblem was originally a black cross on a white background, but in the 14th century the gold cross of Jerusalem and the arms of the Holy Roman Empire were conferred on it by the Grand Master of the Teutonic Order.

[1] See *Dubbing ceremonies* page 48.

Templars, and many others. Together they made up what was in fact a standing ecclesiastical army. The crusades fought against European heretics led to more military orders being created, for example the Militia of Jesus, the Cross-Bearers, and others.

Decline and renaissance

In the 12th century it was the hereditary character of the enfeoffed knighthood, with all its laws and its privileges, that dominated the age.

In the 13th century the 'courtly' spirit flourished, and the noble lady was made the object of an unbounded devotion that sometimes extended to worship on a quite ridiculous scale. In support of this we quote the incident of the Welsh knights who were so convinced that love triumphed over all that they braved a harsh winter wearing clothing so light they froze to death at the feet of their ladies!

The 14th century saw a more or less universal return to the mood of rapaciousness of the previous century which drove many knights to leave their battle line in order to capture a rich prisoner and hold him to ransom. And what scorn they showed towards the lower classes! 'The peasant is a pig and he lives like a pig. . . . No-one should pity a peasant when his lord makes him starve or breaks his arms and legs' – so wrote a gentle trouvère[1] who must have had a narrow escape from the avenging pitchforks of a Pastoureau or a Jacques.[2] All that the undisciplined nobility retained of the ideals of chivalry (which they had exalted to an even greater degree) was arrogance, and this arrogance was to lead them to disaster. The sense of honour that survived in some commanders made them on occasion abandon a favourable position in order to fight in open country, or scorn a flank attack in preference for the 'straight road' and thus lead their troops to the slaughter. On

[1] North of the Loire the trouvères were the equivalent of the troubadours of the land of Oc and the German *Minnesänger*.
[2] Nicknames of the rebel leaders of two of the most violent peasant revolts of the 13th and 14th centuries.

THE BATTLE OF WOERINGEN
The battle of Woeringen (1288), was one of the most important battles of the 13th century to be fought in Western Europe. In it a Belgian prince, John I of Brabant, the champion of communal rights, challenged the German princes, the traditional defenders of feudalism. The latter were led by Siegfried de Westeburg, the archbishop of Cologne, who was levying a much-hated toll on all transport that used the lower reaches of the Rhine. The Duke of Brabant had a political as well as an economic goal, namely to win the succession of Limburg, which was being bitterly contested by a number of claimants. Although outnumbered, the army of John I defeated the enemy coalition because of the unity and discipline of its knights, who charged in serried ranks side by side with the infantry from the town militias of Brussels, Antwerp, Louvain, Tirlemont, Jodoigne, Nivelles, Liège, Clèves and Juliers. The scene portrayed opposite shows Count Henry IV of Luxembourg, who has just thrown aside his sword and lance so as to get a better hold of his sworn enemy, John I of Brabant; the latter is about to receive a mortal blow from a Brabantian knight, Wauthier de Bisdom. (Henry was pretender to the succession of Limburg, whose crest, a red lion, he is wearing.) 'Wretched man,' the Duke was to cry to his saviour, 'you have just slain the most valiant knight on the field!' John I's horse has no emblazoned covering as his original battle-steed had been killed under him shortly before. The repercussions of this battle were enormous. It was celebrated in verse by the poets of the time, in particular by Jan van Heelu, who has left us a vivid account of it in his *Rymkronyk*. The battle secured the full independence of Brabant from the Empire; more importantly perhaps, it was also the first expression of Belgian nationalism. As leader of a powerful state John I henceforth enjoyed a political prestige that would later help to unite all the Belgian territories. The hero of Voeringen was to die needlessly at Bar-le-Duc, in 1296, while taking part in a tournament.

46

the eve of his famous victory at Agincourt in 1415, Henry V demanded of some knights who were setting off on a reconaissance that they should take off their coats of arms, so that when they got back to camp they would not be suspected of turning their backs on the enemy. Yet the same king was to lose his self-control to the extent of ordering the massacre of hundreds of prisoners (seven princes and three hundred bannerets among them) on account of a mere false alarm.

Far worse than that were the sinister changes of fortune that occurred during the struggle between the Houses of Burgundy and Orléans, as recounted by Monstrelet.[1] As he set out to meet his death at the hands of an assassin at Montereau, John the Fearless refused to believe 'that such a lord and prince, the son of the King of France and the successor to his noble crown,[2] would be other than true'. Henry V is reported to have said, by way of a joke, 'War without arson is like sausage without mustard'. And after the massacre of the Swiss garrison at Granson in 1476, Charles the Bold said, 'I'll hang as many as I capture.' Yet the Duke of Burgundy had been raised in the strictest tradition of chivalry.

Already a new kind of chivalry was rising from the ashes of the old.

After the trial of the Templars (1307–1314), the old orders of knighthood were replaced by a new system of royal and nobiliary orders, of which the most famous were the Order of the Garter in England, the Order of the Golden Fleece in Burgundy,[3] and its royal counterpart, the Order of the Holy Ghost, in France.

Dubbing ceremonies

Over the centuries the ancient ceremonies attached to the nomination of a knight became increasingly complex.

KNIGHTS IN THE 14th CENTURY
In the centre of the picture is a bishop wearing his red mitre.
This page of illustrations has been taken from the book entitled *Le Costume et les Armes des soldats de tous les temps*, Volume I (*Arms and Uniforms, Volume I – Ancient Egypt to the 18th century*). Published in 1966, it was – and remains – the first in a series of books that has since grown every year, and it represents a kind of preliminary overview of the vast field which authors Liliane and Fred Funcken are still exploring.
This 'flashback' will be of interest to their readers (or rather, their friends), for it clearly illustrates that the same verve and enthusiasm for uniforms – and the men they ennobled – was present right at the very beginning of the authors' studies into their chosen subject, and in their original concern for strict accuracy for which art, too, is the richer.

(The editor)

---

[1] Enguerrand de Monstrelet was the author, from 1422 to 1424, of a *Chronicle* that continued Froissart's writings.

[2] The Dauphin, the future Charles VII, who was responsible for ordering the assassination.

[3] The statutes of the Golden Fleece make up a veritable code of knightly virtues. This order could only be bestowed on 'gentlemen whose name and prowess are beyond reproach'. Following the marriage of Mary of Burgundy to the Archduke Maximilian, it passed into the House of Habsburg in Spain and Italy.

The squire was ordained in the course of an impressive ceremony consecrated by the Catholic church. The night preceding the ordination was spent in prayer: this was known as the 'Vigil of the Armour'.

The next day the candidate, wearing a brown cassock, made confession, took communion and bathed himself. He then dressed himself in white, lay down and received ceremonial visits.

When this was over he donned his knight's costume, consisting of the coat of mail and the hauberk. Kneeling down, he swore to spare neither life nor possessions in the defence of religion, the widowed, the orphaned and the oppressed. He was shod with a set of golden spurs and presented with a sword and a baldric, or shoulder belt, which he wore around his neck to go to church.

After mass had been said, the priest took the sword, blessed it and gave it back to the novice, who then presented himself to his lord who was seated among his retainers. After kneeling down and swearing a second oath to chivalry, the novice received the 'accolade': he was struck two or three times on the shoulder with the flat of the blade, and was made a knight 'in the name of God, Saint Michael and Saint George'.

Having been duly 'dubbed', the new knight took possession of his helmet, his shield and his lance, then mounted his horse and rode away to show off his newly acquired status to the people of the surrounding district.

The loss of knightly status

Having described the dubbing ceremony, we felt it would be interesting to give an account of the reverse ceremony, which is much less well known.

Any knight convicted of 'treachery, breach of faith or some other abominable capital crime' was hoisted, in full armour, onto a scaffold with his escutcheon fixed upside down to the top of a pole. Twelve priests chanted the vigils for the dead, stopping after every psalm, and at every pause the criminal was divested of a part of his suit of armour, from his helmet

THE 'LANCE', OR TACTICAL UNIT OF THE ARMY
(first half of 14th century)
1. The destrier, or great horse. 2. The knight riding his palfrey or ambling horse. The amble (a kind of easy canter), was one of the least tiring gaits for the rider; it was achieved either by training the animal or by developing its natural tendencies. 3. The squire riding a rounsey. He is carrying the knight's helm, shield and lance; his own helmet, a barbute, is fixed to the back of his saddle. 4. The custrel riding a courser or charger, a kind of fast, powerful palfrey. He is armed with a 'coustille', a weapon halfway between a dagger and a sword which was used to slit the throat of any prisoner who refused to be ransomed. 5. One of the six archers mounted on his curtal and carrying a braquemard, a weapon based on the scimitar. This slightly curved sword also went by the name of 'badelaire', 'basilard', 'baselard' or 'baslard'. 6. The valet mounted on his smaller horse. He is armed with a boar-spear and a badelaire, also called a cutlass. 7. The 'goblet hack', a mare with a special pack-saddle for carrying the knight's provisions. Men-at-arms rode only male horses. 8. The sumpter or baggage horse. 9. Every 'lance' included a varying number of footsoldiers. The two men shown here are armed with the hooked bill (a) and the sackbut (b), weapons which were specially designed to capture important prisoners who would then be held to ransom by their master. The 'lance' was the basic tactical unit of feudal armies from the 10th century onwards. In the mid-15th century this unit still survived as part of the ordinance companies, although on a much more strictly organized basis.

DESTRIER

PALFREY

ROUNSEY

COURSER

COUSILLE

CURTAL

BADELAIRE
CUTLASS

GOBLET
HACK

BRAQUEMARD

SUMPTER

HOOKED BILL

a

b

SACKBUTT

1

2

3

4

5

6

7

8

9

F. FINCKEN

down to his spurs. The escutcheon was disposed of last of all by being broken into three pieces.

The priests intoned the 109th Psalm of David, a terrible series of curses that spared neither the widow, the children nor even the 'iniquitous forefathers' of the fallen knight. Even his prayers were 'imputed to sin'. Then the king or the herald at arms poured a bowl of water over him; this symbolic gesture represented the water of the purifying bath with which his body had once been washed down before his ordination.

After the judgment had been read out, the condemned man was brought down from the scaffold by means of a rope passed round his body. He was then dragged to church on a piece of fencing with a pall draped over it to hear the vigils and the prayer for the dead. He was then handed over to the provost marshal or to the hangman, according to whether he had been condemned by the king's justice to banishment or to death.

The ceremony ended with the herald's proclamation declaring that the children and descendants of the former knight were henceforth 'base-born commoners, not fit to bear arms or to appear at jousts, tournaments, courts or royal assemblies on pain of being stripped naked and beaten with rods, as villeins and offspring of a dishonourable father'.

These proceedings, which were as degrading for the judges as they were for the condemned man, appear to us shrouded in feudal mists. Yet they were carried out against a Captain Franget in the reign of Francis I,[1] at the very height of the Renaissance.

This moribund knighthood, among whom Gaston de Foix and Bayard shone, was soon to disappear under the impact of the first firearms. The quiet courage of the infantryman eventually triumphed over the heroics of the last representatives of the age of chivalry.

THE 'LANCE' IN THE 15th CENTURY
1. The man-at-arms, the leader of the lance. He is wearing a Gothic suit of armour in the Milanese style, weighing 35 kilos. His 'cutting-knife', which is similar to the anelace, hangs from the pommel of his saddle. The mace was also part of the regulation weapons. 2. The man-at-arms' page. His job was to carry his master's lance and act as his valet while learning the art of soldiering. 3. The custrel, a squire who was armed, equipped and provided with a mount at the expense of the leader of the lance. He is carrying an iron half-lance called a 'langue de boeuf' or 'coustille weapon', because of its similarity to the blade of the short sword known as a 'coustille' which was carried by the custrel in fig. 4 on page 51. The latter is often mistaken for the 'langue de boeuf' which is the correct term for the polearm shown here. 4. Three archers on horseback. They used the bow or crossbow, and occasionally the culverin. The type of dagger they are carrying is very similar in appearance to the early cutlass and its near-relations, the 'Catalonian blade' and the 'dagasse'; it is, in fact, an anelace, as shown in (a). (b) is a mail-piercer or cuirass-breaker based on the original misericord, the 'prayer to God' of the English. The sword they are carrying is the 'two-handed' or 'one-and-a-half-handed' type, known also as the 'bastard' or in German called the *anderthalb Hand*; in (c) it is shown hanging from the right side of the saddle pommel. Archers were forbidden to wear pointed shoes ('poulaines'), long spurs, or shoulder padding ('maheutres'). Soldiers carrying missile weapons: 5. The crossbowman. 6. The culverineer. 7. The pikeman. The sword in figs. 5, 6 and 7 is of the type used by footsoldiers, and is called a 'passot' or 'passot sword', or even a 'pass knife' or 'plate knife'; its characteristic feature is the sharp point formed by the angle of the blades. The man in fig. 7 is wearing a boce or bocete, a small shield used in hand to hand fighting, also known as a fist buckler. This 'fully equipped lance' of 1471 could be supplemented by a varying number of subordinate volunteers who wanted to learn the art of soldiering.

---

[1] *Le Vray Théâtre d'honneur*, by Marc Wilson, Lord of La Colombière.

LANGUE de BOEUF

1

ANELACE

2

a

3

4

b

c

5

6

PASSOT

7

BOCE

L. & F. Funcken

Military divisions and their ensigns

The tactical unit: the lance

The collective term 'lance' was used to describe the tactical unit of the feudal army, in which the knight played a key role. The 'lance' could be applied to a varying number of men fighting on foot as well as on horseback.

Several 'lances' combined under the command of a knight banneret formed a 'banner', and a certain number of 'banners' went to make up a 'battle'.

Under Philip Augustus of France, at the beginning of the 13th century, there were between four and six 'lances' to a 'banner'. The 'battle', under the command of one of the feudatories, or great feudal lords,[1] could bring together anything from five to ten 'banners', i.e. 500 to 1,000 horsemen. These figures, however, varied enormously, if only because of the wealth of certain knights banneret who were able to lead a greater than usual number of vassals into war; this is probably what the term 'double bannerets' was used to signify in the 13th century.

Under Philippe de Valois of France, eleven 'battles' assembled 192 'banners' for the battle of Cassel in 1328. The requirements in terms of men must have gradually decreased with time, for in 1452 a certain Lord of Sains received the title of knight banneret on presenting himself for military service, or 'host',[2] with the minimum number of twenty-five men-at-arms.

Curiously enough, the title of banneret was not granted only to knights. There have been instances of squires who were bannerets, and even bannerets who had no title, but whose

[1] One who owned a large fief (*feudatarius*, from *feodum*, a fief).
[2] In French *ost*, from the Latin *hostis* meaning 'enemy', and later 'army'. In feudal times it meant army, or military service due to a suzerain.

ROYAL STANDARDS OF FRANCE
1. Cope standard of Saint Martin, Bishop of Tours during the reign of the Frankish kings from the 6th century onwards. 2. Standard of Charlemagne, King of the Franks and the Lombards. After he was crowned emperor in 800, the standard became scarlet with cocards or (gold), sky blue and or (starting from the centre), with a series of Latin crosses or. 3. Standard of Louis II, the Stammerer (9th century). 4. Standard of Hugh Capet (late 10th century). 5. Standard of Philip Augustus (late 12th century). 6. Oriflamme of Saint-Denis during the reign of Saint Louis (mid-13th century). 7. Standard of John the Good (second half of 14th century). 8. Standard of Charles VII (mid-15th century).

THE JOUST (i) (see page 57)
The joust, often wrongly called the tourney or tournament, opened or closed the mêlée or group combat, or tournament in the correct sense of the word. 1. Jousting knight (late 13th century). The rondel attached to the lance to protect his hand made its appearance at the same period. The equipment specially worn for jousting was confined to a coronal (which replaced the tip of the lance) and to ailettes that pointed forwards so as to deflect blows more readily. 2. Jousting knight (first half of 14th century). Note the saddle, which boxes in the rider at his back and front and has bars across the sides for added safety. 3. Jousting knight (second half of 14th century). The visor of his helmet could only be raised a few centimetres. Apart from the saddle, the equipment is the same as that worn for going into battle. 4. Jousting knight wearing the special helm for use in tournaments (late 14th century). The lance was sometimes as much as 5 metres long. 5. German jousting armour (late 15th century): a) the cord for attaching the shield to the armour (see fig.

skill or financial resources meant they were able to lead a certain number of men to war.

The *banneret* was entitled to wear the hauberk[1] and the double coat of mail.[2]

Immediately below him in rank came the *knight bachelor*, who served under the banner of another because he had not a sufficient number of vassals under him.

The *bachelor*, an ordinary gentleman aspiring to knighthood, was of a lower, less noble status than those just mentioned; he attached himself to a knight under whose aegis he learnt the art of soldiering. Du Guesclin was a bachelor when King Charles V of France appointed him lieutenant-general of his army.

The *squire* accompanied a knight from the time he was fourteen years old until he was made a knight at the age of twenty-one.

Lastly, the *page* worked as an ordinary servant attached to a knight from the age of seven onwards. At the age of fourteen he 'left the ranks of the pages', donned his sword and became a squire.

During the 15th century, in 1445, Charles VII fixed the number of men in a 'lance' said to be 'at full strength' or 'at full complement' at one man-at-arms and his page, a custrel,[3] two archers and a valet. One hundred 'lances' made up one of the twenty 'ordinance companies' which were to turn out to be the core of the new standing army in 1446.

This 'gendarmerie' took in about 9,000 former soldier-brigands from the 'great companies'[4] and was to continue in existence until the 18th century as the gendarmerie of France.[5]

Each company was under the command of a captain, who in

---

[1] Here the term in fact means the hood going down to the shoulders, rather than the actual 'coat' of mail.

[2] This is the habergeon of solid mail, overlapped so as to form a double thickness of armour. See *The hauberk* and *The habergeon* in Part 2.

[3] Custrel, coustilleux or coistrel meant a foot-soldier armed with a half-pike (called a 'langue de boeuf', or a short sword called a 'coustille').

[4] Known also as 'Armagnacs', 'routiers', the '15,000' or '30,000 devils', 'scorchers', 'cutters', 'jostlers', etc., they ravaged France throughout the entire period of the Hundred Years War. The force was chiefly made up of the younger sons or bastards of noble families.

[5] See *Arms and Uniforms – The Lace Wars, Part 1*.

6); b) the poire, or pear-shaped buffer which meant that the shield could slide under the impact of the lance, thereby making the opponent's coronal skid off and greatly reducing the force of the blow; c) the cord holding the 'manifer' (e); d) the lance rest. 6. Side view showing how the shield was fixed to the breastplate (early 15th century). The shield was made from the wood of the lime or pear tree, which was then inlaid with a veneer of very hard polished horn. 7. German jousting armour (late 15th century). 8. When the barrier, or tilt, was in place, the horses had to keep to the correct line; this meant that the maximum angle at which the lances could strike was $75°$, which reduced the force of the impact by at least 25%. 9. When there was no barrier one of the horses could 'cross over', thereby producing a head-on collision in which the speed of each horse added considerably to the force of the impact, as in battle. Jousting without a barrier, which was carried on for a long time in France, became less brutal with the adoption of special type of armour and light or hollow wooden lances. The arms of the jousters, all of whom are Scottish nobles, are as follows: 8. *left* Gordon; 8. *right* Forbes; 9. *left* Leslie; 9. *right* Lindsay.

THE JOUST (ii) (see page 59)
1. Jousting armour from second half of 15th century. This German style of armour was already being worn beyond the Rhine before 1450. The hook-shaped device fixed to the right side of the cuirass was for wedging the heel of the lance and keeping it in a horizontal position without the support of the arm. 1a) Three-quarter back view of the helm showing the method by which it was attached to the backplate of the cuirass. 1b) Position of the head inside the helmet. The side flap could be opened for ventilation. When charging the jouster had to lean his body forward in order to be able to see out of the narrow vision-slit. 2. German jousting helm weighing 9.8 kilos (late 14th century). Note the stud rivets which prevented the coronal of the lance from getting a purchase on the surface of the helm. The brass eyelets are to aid hearing and ventilation. 3. French jousting helm (late 14th

AILETTES

RONDEL

CORONEL

5

POIRE

LANCE REST

d

a

b

c

e

1

2

6

7

3

4

8

9

L. & F. FUNCKEN

many cases had originally served in one of the infamous old bands of soldier-brigands. A son of the Count of Armagnac called the Bastard of Bourbon, William and Anthony de Chabannes, Xaintrailles and La Hire each personally commanded his own company. In the company or ordinanced band of the Duke of Burgundy (see illustrations), the captain was called 'conductor', after the Italian *condottieri*.

The pennon

The pennon (also called 'pennoncel', or 'fane', from the German *Fahne*) decorated the lance of the humblest knight; the latter was sometimes nicknamed 'knight of a single shield' because he was entirely on his own and had no vassals with him. The right to carry this triangular pennant, which was sometimes divided into two points or cornets, was called 'pennonage', and a body of men marching under a pennon was known as a 'pennon'.

Besides its function as a marker, the pennon apparently made the lance easier to handle for the bearer. When the lance was pointed in the direction of an object, the pennon fluttered in the breeze and thereby lightened the weight of the iron shaft; this phenomenon of aerodynamics was called 'giving flight'. It has been claimed that the function of the pennon was to prevent the iron tip of the lance from penetrating too deeply into a wound; however this idea is completely without foundation, and is contradicted by ancient texts which state that the cloth of the pennon often entered the victim's flesh.

The bearer of a pennon had the right to fly a metal replica of the flag from his castle, in place of a weathercock.

The banner

The banner, sometimes called a gonfalon, was the distinguishing mark of a banneret. It was awarded on the actual field of battle in a ceremony that involved cutting off the point of the pennon belonging to the knight who had just been promoted in such a way as to make a right-angled triangle into a right-

century). 4. English jousting helm (early 15th century). 5. Jousting sallet. On the right of the picture the helmet is shown decorated in characteristic fashion. It was no doubt a helmet of this type that inspired Bier the surgeon and Marx the armourer to design the German trench helmet of 1916. 6. Tips of lances used in jousting: a) up to mid-15th century; b) and c) from mid- to late 15th century. These tips were known as coronals. 7. Jouster equipped for the contest of the 'vanishing shield' (second half of 15th century). 8. Details of the helmet and the 'vanishing' shield: a) when this point was struck the shield splintered into eight pieces; b) the release mechanism which was sunk in a shock-absorbent buffer. 9. Sallet with adjustable plates over the forehead; that could be moved by pressing the forked catch (a) (*c.*1470). 10. Sallet with a bevor on a roller (a) used in the 'tail' or 'queue' contest. (b) shows the hole where either a veil (known as a headdress), or a plume of feathers was attached. 11. The roller meant the lower part of the sallet could be slid into position behind the bevor at the moment of charging. 12. Detail of the roller and the clips (a) on which the 'queue' was hung. 13. Jousting knight equipped for the 'queue' contest (second half of 15th century). He is wearing a leg-harness for protection in case he comes into contact with the barrier. The horse is blinkered to prevent any possibility of it shying. 14. Italian armour worn in foot-combat (Milan, *c.*1475). It was called 'tonlet armour' because of the enormous size of its fauld. Part 3 of *The Age of Chivalry* will contain a lengthy sequel to this chapter.

CORONALS

1

1a

1b

2

3

4

5

6

a

b

c

7

8

a

b

9

a

a

10

b

a

11

12

a

a

13

14

R.F. FUNCKEN

PLVS · EST · EN · VOVS ·

angled trapezium, or an isosceles triangle into an isosceles trapezium, depending on the shape of the pennon. This cutting up of the flag was done with great ceremony and was known as 'making a banner from a pennon'; the new banneret was awarded the informal title of 'knight of the square banner'. Between 1310 and 1350 the banner became square in shape.

A banneret setting out for war was said to be 'putting out his banner'; he 'rehoisted his banner' when he took up his position once more after a period of absence in which poverty had prevented him from maintaining the requisite number of men-at-arms.

The title of banneret, which was introduced by Philip Augustus of France in the 12th century, disappeared when the ordinanced companies were set up under Charles VII in the 15th century. It is also worth mentioning that the banneret was entitled to choose his own 'war cry', and to wear gold, vair (squirrel), ermine, velvet and scarlet.[1] Another indication of his rank was the banner-shaped weathervane that flew above his castle.

[1] The term 'scarlet' did not mean a particular shade of red but a kind of very fine cloth that could be any colour, even white.

THE TOURNAMENT (i) (see pages 60–61)

1. Stand for the judges. 2. Stands, also called scaffolds, reserved for ladies. 3. Banners of the two knights acting as judges. The two other corners of the lists were decorated with the banners of the squires acting as judges. 4. *Left* banner and great pennon of the challenger (the Duke of Brittany); *right* banner and great pennon of the defender (the Duke of Bourbon). 5. *Left* banners of knights belonging to the party or 'battle' of the challenger; *right* banners of the knights belonging to the defender's party or 'battle'. 6. Knight of honour wearing the headgear which gave him the authority to stop any attack which might have been dangerous against a knight in difficulties; he could do this at any point in the fight at the request of the ladies. 7. Helm worn by the knight of honour. 8. This knight has gossiped about some of the ladies and so has been picked out by them to be 'beaten at the tourney'. After being soundly thrashed, the accused is removed from the mêlée before being trampled on by the horses. 9. Tourneyer who has been penalized for a foul blow. Any knight who struck his opponent when the latter had lost his helm was banished from the tournament and his armour and destrier confiscated. Note that no knight on either side is wearing a hauberk or a mail aventail. The second knight from the right is wearing a very striking sallet which already anticipates the morion that appeared at the end of the 16th century. These aptly-named 'trépignées' (literally, a trampling) tended to gather together a much larger number of participants. Sometimes the combat was so fiercely contested that the tourneyers carried on fighting after the end of the tournament, on their way back to their lodgings. This was permitted under the rules of the tournament.

THE TOURNAMENT (ii)

1a) King-of-Arms of the Duke of Brittany, who has received instructions to organize a tournament. He is wearing the coat of arms of the challenger, or appellant, and is holding the tournament sword and the list of knights and squires from which the four judges will be chosen by the defendant. He is also wearing riding boots. 1b) The same King-of-Arms after the defendant has agreed to the combat. On his left shoulder he is wearing a parchment portraying the two lords, the appellant and the defendant, who will lead the tournament. The arms of the judges are shown in the four corners of the parchment; the knights' arms are at the top, with those of the squires below. The parchment is in fact a kind of advertising poster. – The King-of-Arms was chief in the hierarchy of armorial officers. Beneath him came the marshall (though this office was filled only on rare occasions), then the herald and then the pursuivant of arms. 2. A herald with his pursuivant of arms (an aspiring herald) on his left; the latter had the job of proclaiming and sounding the tournament in the name of the King-of-Arms. Three or four similar pairs of officials would accompany the king of arms. Note the trumpeter's flowing sleeves – a style that was to continue in widespread use until the 18th century. 3. One of the four judges with his distinctive white staff, accompanied by his footman, his trumpeter and his pursuivant, who is wearing his coat of arms.

1a   2   3   1b

The royal banner and the oriflamme

As the illustrations show, the royal banner underwent frequent changes in both shape and colour. It was sometimes flown in conjunction with a large pennon – a practice which was also widespread among the great feudal lords.

The oriflamme, which was the ensign and banner of the monks of Saint-Denis, was first carried into battle either by Philip I in the 11th century or by his son Louis VI, called 'the Fat', in the following century. At any rate, it was during the reign of Louis VI that the oriflamme (which was made of red silk and fixed to a gilded shaft – hence its name[1]) was described for the first time.

The oriflamme was lost in 1304 at the battle of Mons-en-Pévèle, where it was captured and torn up by the Flemish. William Guiart, an 'eye-witness' to the event, testified later that the flag which had been destroyed was, in fact, only a copy; and sure enough, the 'real' oriflamme turned up in 1315, under Louis the Hutin. It was seen for the last time at Agincourt, where its bearer, William Martel, lord of Baqueville, lost his life defending it.

THE TOURNAMENT (iii)

1. The Lord of La Gruthuyse dressed for a tournament. He is portrayed in the classic pose of the tourneyer, standing upright in his stirrups and keeping himself balanced by holding on to the handle at the front of his pommel. The wooden club or bludgeon at his side was a much less dangerous weapon than the 'rebated' sword, which had its point and its cutting edge specially blunted. The club was merely used as a prologue to the combat proper, to give the tourneyer a kind of practice run. 2. Tournament helmet: a) taken to pieces; b) reassembled; c) the crest-support made of *cuir bouilli* (moulded leather); d) the crest itself made of stiff parchment or wood. In the original manuscript none of the crests in the form of a civilian headdress or a crown are shown with a turban, or 'tortil'. Here the long floating piece of cloth known as a lambrequin has been cut to a special shape (cf. the lambrequins on the previous page). 3. Three other styles of German tournament helmet from the 15th century. 4. Heavy tournament helmet worn over a bascinet and fitted with a bevor and a leather aventail; this was the style commonly worn in Flanders, Hainault and Germany. 5. Armour for the upper arm and forearm, (a) made of iron, (b) of leather; also shown are three different styles of gauntlet. 6. Light, well-ventilated cuirass known as a 'tonlet' which was usually worn underneath the surcoat. Our drawing here is based on Viollet-le-Duc's own interpretation of the tonlet; however the original manuscript shows a simpler model which is less Gothic in style and has no busk or half-moon tassets. 7. Cover designed to protect the tourneyer's legs and mount during combat: a) outside view; b) inside view. This was concealed under the horse-cloth, or trapper, on which the rider's coat of arms were displayed. The padded bumper, or 'sack', (c) was to protect the horse's breast. The position of the bumper is indicated by the dotted red line in (a); it can be seen in (b).

[1] From the Old French, *orie* (gilded), and *flamme* (flame). Some people justify the name by claiming that the standard itself was decorated with golden stars.

2

a

b

3

c

LAMBREQUINS

d

TRAPPER

1

4

5

TONLET

6

7

a b

a

b

c

SACK

L. & F.
FUNCKEN

The horse and the lance

The horse

We tend to think that the warhorse, the 'destrier' or 'great horse', was enormous in size, because we are working from a completely false notion of the actual weight of a full suit of armour. Nevertheless there is no doubt that the warhorse of the 15th century was a specially bred animal; it was, in fact, the result of a carefully controlled, selective breeding process that aimed to combine the characteristics of the Arab horse with those of the heavily-built European strains.

Excellent results were obtained in France, England, Austria and Germany; however, because of its more aggressive nature, the destrier had a tendency to attack other horses at pasture and to pull its rider rather too 'far forward' for comfort. Its major defect was its lack of stamina; it was unable to maintain a sustained gallop, and its charge was more like a slow canter, or even a trot.

This last-mentioned gait, which was particularly taxing for the rider, was a common form of punishment among the Teutonic knights; it seems that one hour's trotting wearing full armour was a real ordeal for the rider. It is quite understandable, then, that no knight 'got on his high horse' until the last possible moment.

Despite its great strength, the destrier never attained the size of the Ardennais, the Percheron, or the other breeds of Shire or Suffolk horses we are familiar with today.

Shafted weapons: the lance[1]

The lance was the basic weapon of a mounted man-at-arms,

[1] The French word *hast*, and the English *hastated* are both derived from the Latin *hasta*, meaning a lance or shaft. 'Shafted weapon' is the term for any weapon which has its metal part mounted on a long pole.

HERALDRY (i)
A. Tinctures: 1. Gules (red). 2. Purpure (purple). 3. Azure (blue). 4. Vert (green). 5. Sable (black) (from *Sabellis pellis*, a small animal found in large numbers in the area around the holy places; the other possible derivation is the Polish word *sabol*, meaning a sable). 6. Orange or tenné (orange and murrey (purple-red) are used only in British heraldry). The shaded rectangles show the conventional hatchings used for black and white illustrations. B. Metals: 1. Or (gold). 2. Argent (silver). C. Furs: 1. Ermine. 2. Ermines. 3. Vair. 4. Counter-vair. 5. Counter-vair in Pale. 6. Vairy. 7. Counter-vairy. D. The principal partitions: 1. Party per pale. 2. Party per fess. 3. Party per bend. 4. Party per bend sinister. 5. Quarterly. 6. Party per saltire. 7. Gyronny. 8. Tierced in pale. 9. Tierced in fess. 10. Tierced in bend sinister. 11. Tierced in bend. 12. Tierced in chevron. 13. Tierced in pall. 14. Tierced in pile reversed. 15. Tierced in cross quarter-pierced. 16. 8 quarters. 17. 16 quarters. 18. Heraldic representation of Henry VI of England in his tournament armour, taken from the *Armorial equestre de l'Europe et de la Toison d'or* (c.1450). The artist has portrayed his subject in a stylized fashion so as to make the armorial bearings easy to identify. In doing so he has omitted none of the essential pieces of tournament equipment, which will be shown in detail later in the appropriate plates. Note, however, the monarch's foot sticking out from beneath the trapper. He is wearing a soleret with a poulaine, the pointed end of which has been 'rebated' in order to prevent accidental injury.

HERALDRY (ii) (see page 69)
E. The Honourable Ordinaries: 1. Chief. 2. Base or point. 3. Pale. 4. Fess. 5. Bend. 6. Bend sinister. 7. Dexter flank. 8. Sinister flank. 9. Bordure. 10. Cross. 11. Saltire. 12.

and was made from the wood of the ash, hornbeam, fir or apple-tree. During the Middle Ages it was often called a 'glaive' (from the Greek *klados*, meaning stick or branch). Together with the sword, the lance was the weapon of Norman freemen; however the wealthy mounted warriors of previous centuries, who were future knights in embryo, were not above using it – far from it, in fact.

According to Viollet-le-Duc and several modern authors, the lance was first used in a horizontal position, tucked under the arm, during the 12th century; this was the date of the invention of the pommel, which provided the rider with a firm support in the saddle. There are, however, many illustrated documents from the 8th, 9th, 10th and 11th centuries which testify to the opposite being the case.

Even more useful as evidence is the bas-relief of the cathedral of Saint Peter of Angoulême[1] (used by Viollet-le-Duc in support of his argument). This quite clearly shows a knight holding his lance under his arm rather than at arm's length: he has struck his opponent with such force that the latter has lost his stirrups and is toppling over, pierced through.

When he was in position, cleaving to his galloping horse and leaning well forward with his lance firmly wedged under his arm, the horseman of feudal times could pierce even the stoutest byrnie. Only the invention of plate armour made it necessary to fit a cantle to the saddle to provide a firm support for the rider's back and to give more 'thrust' to the lance (now longer, heavier and reinforced with a specially-designed 'armour-piercing' point[2]).

Before this period the straight, light shaft was used in exactly the same way as by lancers from the time of the First Empire to World War I, that is wedged under the arm during a charge or held at arm's length like a javelin during hand-to-hand fighting.

As the lance grew thicker, its diameter had to be reduced at the place where it was held in the hand. The small iron rondel,

Chevron. 13. Pall. 14. Gusset. 15. Orle. 16. In escutcheon. 17. Quarter. 18. Quarter voided. 19. Canton. 20. Lozenge. 21. Pile reversed. 22. Pile. 23. Pile issuing from the dexter. 24. Pile issuing from the sinister. *25. Mantel. 26. Gyron. *27. Emmanche. *28. Pile. F. Diminutives of partitions and ordinaires: 1. Paly. 2. Barry. 3. Bendy sinistery. 4. Bendy. 5. Paly of 9. 6. Barry of 11. 7. Bendy sinistery of 13. 8. Bendy of 13. 9. Gemelly. 10. Per pale and barry. 11. Per bend and bendy sinistery. 12. Per fess and paly. 13. Pallets fitched. 14. Three chevrons. 15. Chevronny. 16. Chevron reversed engrailed. 17. Fretty. 18. Lozengy. 19. Fusilly. 20. Chequy. 21. Barry nebuly. 22. Fess indented in base. 23. Fess dancetty. 24. Fess counter-embattled. 25. Fess betressed and counter-betressed. 26. Fess embattled and counter-embattled. 27. Fess embattled. 28. Fess fusilly. 29. Bend engrailed and counter-engrailed. 30. Pale fitchy. 31. Bend couped. 32. Chevron couped. 33. Bordure. 34. Bordure engrailed. 35. Orle. 36. Bordure compony. 37. Per fess dancetty. 38. 3 bars wavy. 39. 3 batons in pale. 40. Tressure flory and counter-flory. 41. Cross potent. 42. Cross cleché voided. 43. Cross moline. 44. Cross patée. 45. Philip the Good, Duke of Burgundy, the founder, first leader and sovereign of the Order of the Golden Fleece. Arms: Quarterly, 1 and 4 semé-de-lys or within a bordure compony argent and gules (Burgundy modern); 2 bendy of 6 or and azure within a bordure gules (Burgundy ancient) impaling sable a lion rampant or armed and langued gules (Brabant); 3 Burgundy ancient impaling argent a lion rampant queue-fourché gules crowned and armed or, langued azure (Limburg); overall an inescutcheon or charged with a lion rampant sable armed and langued gules (Flanders). 46. Guillaume de Vienne, seigneur of Saint-Georges and bailiff-general of Burgundy. At the foundation of the Order of the Golden Fleece in Bruges in 1429 he received the second position in the Order (the first being reserved for his sovereign). Arms: gules an eagle or.
* Translator's note: as nos. 25, 27 and 28 are found in French heraldry, but not in British, the French terms have been left.

---

[1] The frieze dates from the 12th century and is situated to the right of the main portal.
[2] Spearheads will be dealt with in Part 3 of *The Age of Chivalry*.

E

F

45

46

L. & F. Funcken

in effect a kind of shield protecting the hand, had been invented a hundred years earlier, at the end of the 13th century. Henceforth the lance was too heavy to be carried under the arm and supported by the strength of the muscles alone, and so from the end of the 14th century onwards it was suspended from a kind of small hook fixed to the cuirass. From the mid-15th century it was supported by a much larger attachment that was initially a permanent fixture but later was designed to fold away. This support was, and still is, on occasion, called a 'faucre', it is, in fact, the cuirass rest, and is often confused today with the lance rest.[1]

HERALDRY (iii)

G. Charges: 1. Bezants. 2. Torteaux. 3. Billets. 4. Fusils. 5. Annulets. 6. Crescents. 7. Mullets. 8. Mullets of 12 points. 9. Comet in pale. 10. Cinquefoils. 11. Trefoil. 12. Coquerelle. 13. Grenadine. 14. Thistles. 15. Rose. 16. Lion rampant. 17. Lion rampant to the sinister. 18. Lion rampant coward. 19. Lion passant. 20. Lions addorsed. 21. Lions combattant. 22. Leopard. 23. Leopard lionné. 24. Eagle. 25. Eaglets. 26. Alerions. 27. Gryphon. 28. Dragon. 29. Unicorn. 30. Horse. 31. Bear. 32. Boar. 33. Boar's head. 34. Pascal lamb. 35. Bull's head. 36. Squirrel. 37. Greyhound. 38. Bull. 39. Dolphin. 40. Chabots. 41. Bars addorsed. 42. Chimera. 43. Mermaid. 44. Moor's head. 45. Dexter hand. 46. Dexter arm and sword. 47. Clasped hands. 48. Oak tree issuing from a mound. 49. Orange-tree eradicated. 50. Olive-tree. 51. Tree eradicated. 52. North wind. 53. Martlets. 54. Ducks. 55. Doves. 56. Raven. The reader will find some charges in addition to the 56 shown here in the following arms of the knights of the Golden Fleece. Knights of the Golden Fleece: 57. Jean de Roubaix. Ermine a chief gules. His bizarre-looking crest represents a pair of armoured legs. 58. René Pot. Quarterly, 1 and 4 azure a fess or (Pot); 2 and 3 chequy argent and sable. 2 belts gules buckled or supporting 2 swords in scabbard gules, hilts, chapes and studs all or, in bend one over the other (Courtejambe). 59. Roland d'Uytkerke. Argent a cross sable charged with 5 escallops or. 60. David de Brimeu. Quarterly, 1 and 4 argent 3 eagles gules, armed and membered azure (Brimeu); 2 and 3 argent a bend gules (Mingoral). 61. Hugues de Lannoy. Argent 3 lions rampant vert, crowned or, armed and langued gules, within a bordure engrailed of the last. His younger brother appears on the following page (fig. 3). 62. Jean de Commines. Gules a chevron or between 3 escallops argent within a bordure of the second.

---

[1] The lance, lance rest and cuirass rest will be dealt with in Part 3 of *The Age of Chivalry*.

G

1
2
3
4
5
6
7
8
9
10
11
12
13
14

15
16
17
18
19
20
21
22
23
24
25
26
27
28

57

58

59

L.&F.
IUNCKEN

60

61

62

29
30
31
32
33
34
35
36
37
38
39
40
41
42

43
44
45
46
47
48
49
50
51
52
53
54
55
56

Jousts and tournaments

Knightly sports developed very early on as a result of a combination of factors, namely a natural inclination towards weapons and feats of military valour, a need for regular training and a desire to show off one's skill and physical prowess in public.

The joust, a combat between two horsemen armed with lances, must certainly have been the earliest known form of these courtly fights, if only because it was the simplest. The use of special tips for the lances and light shafts that would break more easily was probably common practice in these early jousts, since it is hard to imagine how a knight wanting to train at the same time as practise a violent sport would have failed to take this basic precaution – regardless of how anxious he was to show off his skill.

Nevertheless it is clear that combats of this kind took on quite a different aspect when the opponents involved allowed personal grudges to enter into things. This must have been quite a common occurrence, yet even in this situation the rules of jousting and chivalry laid down that only the helmet or the shield could be struck. What is far more likely to have happened is that two deadly enemies chose a more private place in which to settle their quarrel – always assuming they did not turn the honourable institution of the duel into a common ambush! It would be a grave mistake to take too exalted a view of chivalry; this same epoch which is celebrated in so many courtly romances was riddled with instances of base or dishonourable conduct.

The illustrations trace the development of the joust through the Middle Ages and the gradual process of refinement it underwent. Indeed it went too far in this direction, at the same time going to greater and greater lengths to ensure the safety of the combatant, until by the end of the 15th century he was

HERALDRY (iv)

1. Antoine de Toulongeon. Quarterly, 1 and 4 gules 3 bars wavy or; 2 and 3 gules 3 gemels argent, all within a bordure of the last. 2. Jean de la Trémouille. Or a chevron gules between 3 eagles azure armed and membered of the second, within a bordure of the second. 3. Gilbert de Lannoy. Argent 3 lions rampant vert, crowned or, armed and langued gules, within a bordure engrailed of the last, debruised by a label of three points azure. 4. Jean de Luxembourg. Argent a lion rampant queue-fourché gules, crowned and armed or, langued azure, debruised by a label of 3 points of the last. His crest represents a dragon's head with a scarlet tongue. 5. Jean de Villiers de L'Isle-Adam. Or a chief azure charged with a dexter arm vested ermine supporting a pendant of the last over all. 6. Antoine de Croÿ. Quarterly, 1 and 4 argent 3 adzes gules (Renty); 2 and 3 argent 3 bars gules (Croÿ). 7. Robert de Mamines. Azure a lion rampant or, armed and langued gules, charged with a fleur-de-lys of the last. 8. Jacques de Brimeu. Argent 3 eagles gules armed and membered azure, debruised by a demi-lion naissant of the second. 9. Pierre de Bauffremont. Quarterly, 1 and 4 vairy or and gules (Beauffremont); 2 and 3 gules 3 cinquefoils pierced or (Vergy); over all an inescutcheon gules charged with 3 escutcheons argent (Charny). 10. Philippe de Ternant. Chequy or and gules. His crest represents a woman with hands clasped.

The Order of the Golden Fleece was founded in Bruges on February 10th, 1429, and placed under the divine patronage of the Virgin Mary and Saint Andrew. It originally had a membership of thirty-one knights which excluded any Frenchman who was a subject of the King of France. On the death of Charles the Bold in 1477 the position of Grand Master fell to Maximilian of Austria, the husband of Mary of Bur-

encased in a kind of blockhouse. By this time jousting had more or less developed into a sport, and it was doubtless as a reaction against this process of 'bourgeoisification' that some young German contestants invented the 'pan' or 'grill' race. This involved jousting bare-headed, wearing no armour but with a grid tied to the chest: this was the 'pan' or the 'grill' which had to be knocked off by the iron tip of the lance – with what fatal risks one can easily imagine! It was customary, moreover, to place an open coffin in the lists before the combat started.

Jousting, which was very popular with the spectators, usually marked the beginning or end of a tournament. When not part of a tournament these confrontations were called 'great and plenary jousts, open to all comers'.

Of course the actual art of handling a lance was learned away from these dangerous ceremonial occasions. Jousting was practised against a quintain, or a dummy armed with a shield and a mace. If it was not struck correctly it spun round and dealt the rider a glancing back-handed blow.

The tournament, which was also called the 'tourney', is generally thought to have originated in France. In the 9th century, the historian Nithard, who was Charlemagne's grandson, described a tournament held in Strasbourg around 842 in which two equal parties of Saxons, Basques, Austrasians and Bretons met one another. However, a reference to a similar encounter in Barcelona, as far back as 811, has been recorded, and most major tournaments between the 10th and 12th centuries were in fact held in Germany, where they are said to have been organized by Henry the Fowler (876–936).

The brutal developments that had taken place in tournaments so often had fatal consequences that in the 9th century Pope Eugene II anathematized them. His successors followed suit: Innocent II, Eugene III, and Alexander III in the 12th century, Innocent IV in the 13th and Clement V at the beginning of the 14th century, excommunicated all 'tourneyers' and forbade the burial of victims in consecrated ground. It made no difference, however, and the slaughter continued, despite the strict set of rules laid down by Geoffroy de Preuilly at the beginning of the 11th century.

gundy. On the collar of the order was a picture showing a whetstone striking a flint, inscribed with the motto 'Ante ferit quam flamma micet' (He strikes before the flame shoots up). Also depicted was the golden fleece, taken from the legend of Phrixos who sailed across the seas on the back of a ram with golden fleece. After his journey he hung the fleece in the temple of Colchides, where it was stolen by the Argonauts.

HERALDRY (v)

1. Frédéric, Count of Meurs. Quarterly, 1 and 4 sable a double-headed eagle argent, armed and membered or (Saarwerden); 2 and 3 or a fess sable (Meurs). 2. Simon de Lalaing. Gules 10 lozenges argent, 3, 3, 3 and 1, the first debruised by a lioncel gules. 3. Jean de Melun. Azure 7 bezants, 3, 3 and 1; a chief or. 4. Jacques de Crèvecoeur. Gules 3 chevrons or. 5. Jean de Vergy. Gules 3 cinquefoils pierced or within a bordure argent. 6. Guy de Pontailler. Gules a lion rampant or, armed and langued azure. 7. Baudot de Noyelles. Gules 3 gemels argent, debruised by a label of 3 points of the last. 8. Jean de Luxembourg, bastard son of Hautbourdin. Argent a lion rampant queue-fourché gules, crowned and armed or, langued azure, debruised by a bendlet of the last. 9. Charles of Burgundy, Count of Charolais. Arms of Burgundy (see Philip the Good), debruised by a label of 3 points argent. 10. Thibaud de Neuchâtel. Gules a bend argent. All these knights were captains or commanders who had led men into battle and had honours and riches heaped upon them by their seigneur. Some of them died in combat, like Jean de Villiers, Robert de Mamines and Thibaud de Neuchâtel. Hugues de Lannoy, the veteran of the Order, died at the age of seventy-two. The most fearless 'jouster and tourneyer' of them all was Simon de Lalaing; one of his many famous opponents was Charles of Burgundy, who successfully fought against him at the age of eighteen. As for Jean de Luxembourg, he was beheaded on the orders of Louis XI. The Knights of the Golden Fleece fought against the troops of Flanders, Liège, England and France, and even, on occasion, against the Turks and the Tartars.

L. & F. FUNCKEN

The names of the most famous victims of this dangerous passion have been preserved in medieval chronicles. Geoffrey de Magneville, Count of Essex, killed in 1216: Florent, Count of Hainault and Philip, Count of Boulogne, both killed in 1223: the Count of Holland in 1234: Gilbert of Pembroke in 1241: Hermand de Montigny in 1258: John of Brandenburg in 1269 and John, Duke of Brabant, in 1294. In 1240, at the tournament of Nuys, near Cologne, sixty knights and squires perished, trampled or crushed to death by their horses. The most deplorable incident of all was the death of William Montagu, who was killed by his own father in 1382. Yet alongside these unfortunates a breed of experts was already evolving who can be likened to the tennis champions of today. These men travelled all over Europe winning fame and fortune simply by virtue of their skill at this dangerous sport. In the 13th century William Marshall, who was to be regent of England during the minority of Henry III, amassed considerable wealth by this method.

Following the example of the Popes, monarchs themselves banned tournaments on occasion, though only for a limited period. In England they were proscribed by Henry II during the 12th century and then restored by his successor, Richard I. In 1299, they were again banned by Edward I, despite the fact that he himself had led eighty knights to the tournament at Châlons in 1274. They reappeared in even greater strength during the reign of Edward III, who issued safe-conducts to any Frenchmen willing to meet his knights in courtly combat. (This, incidentally, took place at the height of the Hundred Years War, two years before Edward inflicted a crushing defeat on the French at Crécy, in 1346). The famous Order of the Garter was to be created shortly afterwards, in the course of another great tournament.

In France both Philip the Fair and Philip the Long prohibited tourneys, in 1313 and 1318 respectively; their opposition to them was reinforced by the fact that a custom had grown up of consecrating the victor of a tournament a knight, which was regarded as an unacceptable slur on a noble institution.

POLEARMS (i)

War hammers (depending on the relative size of the spike, the hammer was called a 'bec de perroquet', a 'bec d'oisel', a 'bec de faucon' or a 'bec de corbin'): 1. English (1420). 2. German (second half of 15th century). 3. German (late 15th century). 4. German (late 14th century). 5. French (second half of 15th century). 6. French (mid-15th century). 7. Swiss (15th century). 8. French (late 15th century). 9. Hussite (15th century). 10. German (mid-15th century). 11. French (late 14th century). 12. French (mid-15th century). 13. French (15th century). 14. German (14th-15th century). 15. English (late 14th century). 16. French; known as a maul or plummet (late 14th century). 17. French; known as a 'picois' (1350). 18. French; known as a 'plummet' (1440). 19. Italian (1480). 20. German (15th century). The weapons in figs. 7, 8, 13, 16, 17 and 18 were all mounted on long shafts and used solely by footsoldiers. Military maces: 21. English (1470). 22. German (second half of 15th century). 23. English (1300). 24. French (mid-15th century). 25. French (late 14th century). 26. French (late 12th century). 27. English (mid-15th century). 28. German (14th century). 29. French (early 15th century). 30. French (late 15th century). Despite their relatively small size and simple design, these weapons were far more deadly than the sword or the lance. Constant efforts were made to have them banned, as they were able to buckle or stave in the strongest armour with deadly effectiveness. They continued to be used in battle until the pistol appeared on the scene. We are left wondering at these vain but repeated attempts to have the mace banned – attempts made, moreover, by knights, warriors *par excellence* who would have been expected to be more interested in the effectiveness of a weapon. The bludgeon, a variation on the mace (fig. 26), also remained popular despite the conventions that dominated feudal society until the 13th century.

Military flails: 31. German (15th century). 32. Hussite (15th century). 32a) This weapon, known as a 'scorpion' in France and England, had spiked iron weights on the end of its chains. It was also used in

1

2

3

4

5

6

7

8

9

PAVISE

10

11

12

13

14

15

17

PICOIS

6

MAUL or
PLUMMET

18

PLUMMET

19

20

BLUDGEON

21

22

23

24

25

26

27

28

29

30

31

32

32b

SCORPION

32a

32c

33

34

35

36

37

38

39

40

41

The rules and rituals of these warlike occasions grew more complicated as time went on. The increasing influence of women resulted in the dangers being greatly reduced and the tournament being transformed into an exhibition of gallantry as much as a display of sporting prowess by the 15th century. Our double-page illustration depicts the main features of the tournament.

Heralds and Kings-of-Arms

Heralds first appeared during the reign of Philip Augustus, when their function was to proclaim the name of the victor at tournaments; they had no official status until they were entered in the royal accounts in 1285, and no strict hierarchy or clearly-defined function until the 14th century.

The herald was generally chosen after a battle from among a group of apprentices known as the 'pursuivants', and received his title after the heralds and Kings-of-Arms had cast their votes. The newly promoted herald was then given a special name connected with a particular town, fortress or province: thus we find examples of names like 'Jerusalem', 'Leicester', 'Windsor', 'Agincourt', 'Guyenne', 'Navarre' and 'Berry'. During his apprenticeship, however, the 'pursuivant' was called after the armorial bearings of his lord, for example 'Vert-Eagle', or 'Crescent'.

The main tasks of the herald were to keep a roll of the nobility, study and teach the art of heraldry, and devise new armorial bearings. He was indispensable at even the smallest tournament, but his heraldic knowledge came in even more useful on the battlefield, where he could identify the noble victims among the fallen.[1]

The King-of-Arms, who was the principal figure in the hierarchy, was responsible for one of the heraldic marches into which the kingdom was divided. These districts (there were eighteen in France in 1396, eight in 1420 and fifteen in 1455) each contained a variable number of 'heraldries'.

[1] After Crécy three heralds and two secretaries drew up a list of eleven French princes and 1,200 knights who had been killed in the battle.

Flanders and northern France, where it was known as a war stirrup. 32b) Head of a battle whip. 32c) Head of a chain plummet. 33. French (12th century). 34. German (mid-15th century). 35. French (early 15th century). 36. Hussite (15th century). 37. Swiss (15th century). 38. French (14th century). 39. German (mid-15th century). 40. Swiss; this had a rod or swivelling bar on the end of its shaft. We are often shown spectacular flails in films and books that have long chains with fearsome-looking maces swinging on the end of them. In fact these chains were never more than three-quarters the length of the shaft, in case the mace swung back and struck the hand of the person wielding it. In England this weapon was wryly nicknamed a 'holy water sprinkler'. 41. 'Pavised' foot-soldier (shielded by a pavise) armed with a hammer with a hand-guard and a long spike (1440).

FLEMISH TOWNSMEN OF THE 13th CENTURY
1. Footsoldier armed with a *goedendag* (the name meant 'good day' in Flemish). This was a rather callous nickname for a sapling with a spike and a ferrule on the end, a type of polearm that was as easy to assemble as it was effective. The *goedendag* was described by Froissart in his *Chronicles* and depicted in the frescoes of the Leughemeete, though its name was often written 'godenda', 'god-endac' or 'godendart'. It was the subject of many arguments among military writers: some claimed it was a type of halberd, while others thought it was a development of the voulge. 2. Soldier of the town militia of Ghent; he is a member of the guild of cloth-shearers. There have been many accounts of the townsmen 'carrying a little of their native soil to their lips' just before the start of the famous battle of Courtrai. This ritual most probably involved their putting a small piece of earth in their mouths as a token of their acceptance of the sacrifice they were about to make in the face of an enemy who were determined to give no quarter. 3. Townsman from Alost. 4. Standard-bearer from the guild of Bruges butchers. 5. Knight fighting on foot with a shortened lance. The small number of cavalry present at the battle has often led

GOEDENDAG

It is worth making the point that these experts were in fact all typical of their kind, in that they made a great many mistakes without contributing much in other respects to the advancement of heraldry.

writers to the (false) conclusion that both the burghers and the nobles deserted the town armies on a large scale. 6. Banner of the weavers of Bruges. 7. The banner of Flanders, which was entrusted to the charge of an outstandingly brave knight. The heroic Robert of Artois is said to have snatched a piece of it before falling beneath the blows of a lay brother and a Carmelite friar at the battle of Courtrai. 8. Town banner of Ghent. The standard-bearer was both a knight and a member of the burgher class. 9. Banner of Ypres. 10. Crossbowman. Along with the archers in the army, this type of soldier enjoyed a reputation for great skill. The bowman shown here is wearing the arms of Jean de Namur who, along with many others like Jean de Renesse, Guillaume de Juliers and Henri de Lonchin, had flocked to the side of the Flemish for the battle of Courtrai. The town militias played a decisive role in political life from the 13th century onwards. Those from the principality of Liège, in particular, opposed the territorial ambitions of Henry V of Germany, the Count of Namur, Henry the Blind and lastly, Henry I, Duke of Brabant. In their turn the Brabantian militias of Jean I, the protector of the townsmen's rights, were to wrest Limburg away from the domination of the German princes, the last champions of feudalism. Later Flanders was to rise up against French domination and crush the army of Philip the Fair at Courtrai in the famous battle of the Golden Spurs, in 1302. However the reputation for military valour enjoyed by the town militias was somewhat exaggerated; they lacked unity, training and discipline, and tended to conquer their opponents by sheer weight of numbers alone. When confronted by a flexible adversary and increasingly sophisticated artillery, they simply went from one disaster to the next: the Flemish defeats at Cassel in 1328, and at the siege of Tournai in 1340, were followed by those of the Liégois

at Waleffe in 1347 and the Brabantians in 1372; the Flemish lost again outside Oudenarde in 1379, at Nevele in 1381 and finally at Roosebeke in 1382, where the French army of Philip the Bold was to set the seal on the decline of the townsmen as a force for once and for all. The final attempts of the townsmen to defend their democratic rule were paid for in terrible massacres: the defeats sustained at Othée in 1408 and Gavre in 1453 by the towns of Liège and Ghent respectively, the defeat of Dinant in 1466, then the final crushing of the townsmen of Liège at Brusthem in 1467, and at Liège itself in 1468.

POLEARMS (ii)

1–3. Military scythes of the 14th century. These very rudimentary weapons, which consisted of a scythe blade fitted at an angle of 180° to the shaft, did not originate in any one specific country. These makeshift polearms were the weapons used in the first popular revolts.
Slash-hooks: 4. Swiss (14th century). 5. and 6. French; also known as 'couteaus de brèche' (15th century). 7. English; known as a 'langue de boeuf' or 'langdebeve' (15th century). The original agricultural implement, which survived only until the last years of the 14th century, has changed almost beyond recognition into an instrument of war. The development was marked by the new names it acquired in the process, which were evidently thought to be more suitable than words like 'slash-hook' that betrayed the peasant origins of the weapon.
Guisarmes: 8. French (late 14th century). 9. French; also known as a 'goyard' (early 15th century). 10. Italian; known as a 'glaive-guisarme' (15th century). 11. English; known as a 'glaive-guisarme' (late 15th century). 12. French; known as a 'bédoil' or 'bedouche' (early 14th century). 13. Swiss (13th century). 14. Swiss (late 15th century). 15. Swiss (mid-15th cen-

tury). 16. English (second half of 15th century). 17. Italian (mid-15th century). 18. English (second half of 15th century). 19. Swiss (late 15th century).
Voulges: 20. Swiss (1300). 21. German (mid-14th century). 22. German (second half of 14th century). 23. Swiss (second half of 14th century). 24. French (late 14th century). The voulge, which was obviously a descendant of the plough-share, developed into a more elaborate weapon, as did the military scythe. A spike was added to it and from then on it continued gradually evolving until it ended up as the familiar halberd. In our opinion this process of change came to a halt when the head, with its tip, its axe and its spike, was made in a single piece.
Halberds: 25. French (early 15th century). 26. German (first half of 15th century). 27. Swiss (first half of 15th century). 28. and 29. German (mid-15th century). 30. German (second half of 15th century). 31. German (late 15th century).
Boar-spears and courseques: 32. English boar-spear (15th century). 33. Italian boar-spear (15th century). 34. German corseque (15th century). 35. Burgundian corseque (15th century). 36–38. Italian corseques (15th century). The corseque, or corsesque, was called a chauvesouris when its lugs were turned upwards and notched (fig. 37); when its lugs turned downwards it was sometimes called a roncone. These arms are the forerunners of the 'pertuisane' of the later centuries (see Part 3), although the weapon in fig. 34 was known as a partisan in 15th century Germany.
Military forks: 39. Hussite (15th century). 40. 1450. 41. German (15th century).
Long infantryman's axes: 42. 1250. 43. 1260. 44. German (late 14th century). 45. German (15th century). 46. and 47. Swiss (15th century). 48. German (15th century). 49. Scottish (15th century). 50. 1450. 51. Mid-15th century.
Cavalryman's axes: 52. 1200. 53. 1400. 54. Turkish (late 15th century). 55. 15th century. 56. First half of 15th century. 57. Second half of 15th century. 58. 1470. 59. and 60. Late 15th century.

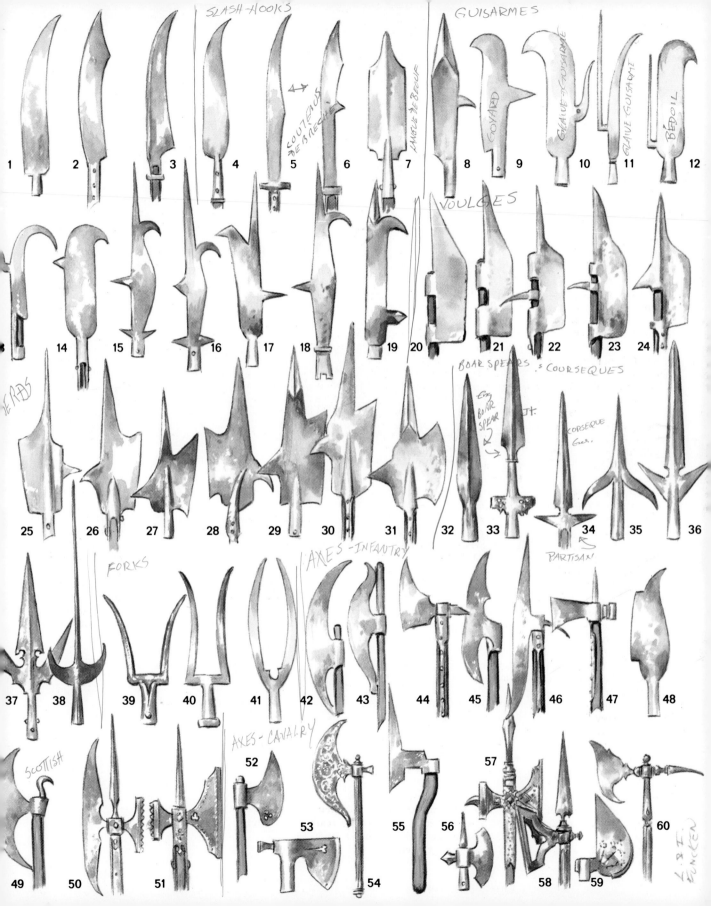

SLASH-HOOKS

GUISARMES

COUTEAUS DE BRECHE

LANGUE DE BŒUF

GOYARD

GLAIVE-GUISARME

GLAIVE GUISARME

BÉDOIL

VOULGES

SE BAS

BOAR SPEARS & COURSEQUES

Eng BOAR SPEAR

It.

KORSEQUE Ger.

PARTISAN

FORKS

AXES-INFANTRY

AXES-CAVALRY

SCOTTISH

1   2   3   4   5   6   7   8   9   10   11   12
14   15   16   17   18   19   20   21   22   23   24
25   26   27   28   29   30   31   32   33   34   35   36
37   38   39   40   41   42   43   44   45   46   47   48
49   50   51   52   53   54   55   56   57   58   59   60

L. & F. FUNCKEN

Heraldry

Heraldry, or the art of blazoning, was for a long time considered the most important of the sciences. It rapidly evolved a strange vocabulary of its own – a technical language whose jargon discourages the layman but makes it possible for any amorial bearing to be described in words.

In the 12th century, the participants in a joust or a tournament displayed their coat of arms on their shields, then, in the following century, on the crests of their helmets. The first book a gentleman would have in his library would most definitely be a treatise on heraldry, and even the common people could identify their heroes as easily, if not more easily, as today's football fan recognizes the colours of his favourite team.

The vocabulary of heraldry was particularly well developed in France, since this was the land of the tournament *par excellence*; it was adopted by the other European nations, all of whom, however, had their own customs and traditions. Thus the sacrosanct rule forbidding the placing of tincture on tincture, or metal on metal, has frequently been broken, notably in Italy, Germany and Spain.

Our illustrations show a wide range of examples of the different elements that go to make up the coat of arms. It should be noted, however, that several dozen other types of cross are used apart from the few examples we have shown here.

Among the other heraldic 'charges', martlets, bezants and escallops, like simple crosses, are often an indication of a noble lineage going back to the time of the Crusades. There are, in addition, hundreds of less ancient 'charges'.

MEN-AT-ARMS IN THE 14th–15th CENTURIES
1. Uniformed man-at-arms (mid-15th century). 2. Man-at-arms wearing a surcoat (mid-14th century). 3. Man-at-arms wearing an aketon (1370). 4. Man-at-arms in a gambeson and iron breastplate (1400). 5. Man-at-arms wearing an aketon and carrying a dard, or short lance (1420). 6. Man-at-arms in a canvas jack (1425). 7. Man-at-arms in a mail jack and brigandine (1440). 8. Man-at-arms wearing a jack and carrying the small shield known as a boce (1440). The fact he has no leg-armour should not be interpreted as meaning that the wearing of it was forbidden as a general rule; it was entirely a matter of choice for the individual footsoldier. 9. Knight wearing the 'crayfish', a type of decorative surcoat (late 14th century).

III BOWS AND CROSSBOWS

The bow

The bow, which dates back to ancient times,[1] was used as a weapon throughout Europe until the time of the invention of firearms and even after: Cardinal Richelieu, for example, used English mercenary bowmen in the attack on the Ile de Ré in 1627.

Few of the Barbarian peoples used the bow as a fighting weapon since they regarded it as a treacherous weapon,[2] not fit for grown men; this opinion, however, was not shared by the Celts, the Gauls or the Huns, amongst others.

Bows were made in different sizes and in a variety of materials. The most famous of all was the longbow of the English, the true value of which they discovered during the protracted wars they fought against the fierce Welsh. During the campaign of 1280, Edward I created his first body of archers on the lines of the Welsh bowmen. At the same time he greatly improved their tactics, which were limited to ambushes only; Edward substituted for this a method of firing volleys of arrows *en masse*.

Ideally the English bow was supposed to be the same height as the archer himself. In order to determine its size with even greater accuracy, the distance was measured between the tips of the second finger of each hand, with both arms stretched out horizontally. This measurement, which is equivalent to the height of a well-proportioned man, made it possible for those who did not have the correct proportions to arrive at the ideal geometric figure formed by the bow, its string and the arrow at

THE BOW (i)
1. French (10th century). 2. French (9th century). 3. Italian (10th century). 4. Norman (12th century). 5. Norman (11th century). 6. Italian (11th century). 7. Spanish (13th century). 8. German (13th century). 9. French (13th century).
The exact colours of the clothes pictured here must have varied enormously, but were probably mostly in neutral shades. Thus we can feel free to interpret the documentary evidence that is available to us. Fig. 6, for example, is taken from a manuscript from the school of Gerona. The author, who appears to have set about his task with considerable enthusiasm, had only three colours in his palette, namely red, blue and yellow. He has distributed these among the various figures in his illustration with the sole aim of achieving a pleasing aesthetic effect (this includes, incidentally, painting a blue horse!).
In contrast the Spanish miniaturist whose work we used as a source for fig. 7 was more subtle in his effects. He has painted all his archers wearing the same red bonnet, which suggests that this was part of the uniform of their particular calling.

---

[1] Some authors trace its origins back 50,000 years.
[2] Nearer to our own time, the bow of the North American Indians was poor in terms of effectiveness.

the moment of firing. Hence the bow was exactly (one might almost say scientifically) adapted to fit the physical build of the user.

If we add to this personalized method of constructing the weapon an intensive and systematic programme of training, then the result is the perfect archer. This in fact is what happened in England, after a brief period of decline under Edward II. His son Edward III set his people to train intensively, and by the time of his successful expeditions against the Scots in 1331 and 1333 he had a large body of skilled archers at his disposal.

Every citizen had to do target practice with the bow and arrow at the local exercise ground, and young boys copied their elders with an enthusiasm that can easily be imagined; they were each given a bow made to fit their height.

The bow was made out of yew, not the traditional 'good English yew', but the wood of imported yew from Italy and Spain. White elm, hazel, ash and walnut were also used. The oldest existing bow we have been able to discover dates from the beginning of the 13th century and is on display at the British Museum.

As one would imagine, the greatest of care was devoted to the making of arrows.[1]

In France the town of Mâcon was famous for arrow-making.[2] The craftsman was called 'fléchier', or 'flégier', from the French word 'flèche', meaning 'arrow'.

The importance of the bow in the Middle Ages was especially great in Britain; this is borne out by the many surnames still surviving today such as Fletcher ('arrow-maker'), Arrowsmith ('forger of arrowheads'), Bownocker and Stringer ('fitter of bowstrings'), Archer and Bowman ('archer'), and Bowyer ('bowmaker').

THE BOW (ii)
THE GREAT ENGLISH BOW
1. and 2. Breakdown of the various stages involved in stringing a bow. The string was removed by the same procedure, but with the two stages reversed. 3. Firing the bow. When the archer drew the bow back to its full extent he was 'pulling' around 50 kilos. English bowmen (the ones shown here date from the 15th century) in actual fact stood behind their 'anti-cavalry' stakes; here they have been arranged differently so as to provide a clearer view of the figures in action.

Firing the bow: A. At close range. B. At medium range. C. At long range. The red line shows the point the archer is aiming the tip of his arrow at. The white line shows the actual trajectory of the arrow, which would usually cover a distance of around 50 metres before beginning to curve downwards due to the effect of gravity. When firing less than this distance the archer therefore had to aim at a point *below* the target (fig. A). When firing beyond 50 metres, on the other hand, he had to raise the firing angle and aim at a point *above* the target (fig. C). It took years of intensive training for an archer to learn to select the correct point to aim at so as to be able to fire an arrow 'instinctively', with speed and accuracy. Apart from individually aimed shots, the bowman could also fire up into the air, which involved shooting the arrow to a height of 40 or 50 metres at a very steep angle of elevation. After following an oblique trajectory, the arrow would describe a short parabola, then fall vertically to the ground with terrific force of penetration. This method of shooting meant that bowmen could get at the enemy when they were hidden behind their pavises. It was introduced by the English in their French fortresses, and adopted by the French during the 15th century.

---

[1] In England, Norway pine was used in preference to other woods – for example, birchwood.

[2] In French there was a vast range of names for different types of arrows. These included: darde, barbelle, flic, flich, flique, flise, flesse, eslingue, pile, gourgan, passadouz, passador, passadour, passadous, passadoux, sayette, seatte, sognolle, raillon, reiller.

C

B

A

2

3

1

L. & F. Funcken

The archer

The deadly power of even the smallest of our modern light weapons makes us inclined to be a little scornful of the performance of such a simple weapon as the bow, which can be made to appear so spectacularly effective in the hands of film stars. We would be wrong, however, to mock, since for once the film makers have stayed well within the bounds of reality, and from the time of the outbreak of the Hundred Years War (1337–1453) the great English bow went on to earn itself a formidable reputation.

The English archers were to humble the pride of the armour-clad knights of France at Crécy (1346), Poitiers (1356) and Agincourt (1415); they became, and justifiably so, the most feared opponent in Europe. At Crécy in particular, the 6,000 bowmen of Edward III decided the outcome of the battle in a mere ninety minutes of fighting.

This astonishing effectiveness is easily explained when we bear in mind that each archer was picked from among the most reliable and skilful practitioners of this national 'sport'. Moreover each man was able to fire six *individually aimed* arrows a minute up to an effective minimum range of at least 200 yards (about 183 metres); however, the maximum range could be anything up to 400 yards.

This performance, which modern historians have been sceptical about, has been confirmed by an American archer, Dr Saxton Pope,[1] who succeeded in discharging seven arrows before the first one reached the target. In 1924 another American expert, General Thord-Gray, put to shame twelve pistol-shooting champions by successfully hitting a target measuring 66 centimetres in diameter, placed at a distance of 75 metres, with 70 arrows out of 72; the combined score of his opponents was barely within sight of his total. Consequently it is surely not unreasonable to believe previous statements about the skill of crack archers who could hit a human target twelve times in a minute from a range of 200 yards.

[1] His book *Hunting with the Bow and Arrow* (1923) gave a considerable boost to the development of archery in the United States.

THE BOW (iii)
1. German bow, made of oak (13th century). 2. Oriental steel bow (14th century). 3. Italian bow (15th century). 4. Italian steel bow (14th century). 5. French bow with a counter-bend (10th century). 6. French bow (13th century). 7. French bow copied from an oriental or Turkish design (12th century). 8. Idem (14th century). 9. French bow (13th-14th century). This version of the longbow was, it was claimed, more powerful and more accurate than its English rival, which it was intended to supplant. However because of lack of proper training French bowmen never managed to equal the skill of their English adversaries. 10. English longbow (14th century).
Arrows: 11. 15th century arrow, 74 cm in length, from the island of Rhodes. It is of the 'passadoux' type, and has a flat, triangular head. 12. French arrow with a detachable head (15th century). This meant the shaft of the arrow (a) could be easily retrieved. 13. English arrow of the 'dard' type with a heavy socketed head (15th century). A. Cross-section of the fletching or feathering of the arrow.
Arrow-heads: 14. 17. 'Hamstring-cutter' or 'rope cutter' head. Fig. 14 was known as a 'little crescent' and fig. 15 a 'great crescent'. 18. Incendiary arrow-head. Figs. 19–21 and 26–28 all have barbed heads (14th century). Arrows fitted with this type of head were called barbels. Figs. 29–33. *Idem* (15th century). 22, 25, 35, 37–40. These were all armour-piercing heads that could penetrate ordinary coats of mail and cuirasses. Figs. 31 and 38. Arrows that had triangular- or square-faced heads were known as 'boujons', though this term was more commonly applied to a crossbowman's equipment. Socketed heads that fitted over the shaft of the arrow were used until the 15th century, when they were gradually replaced by heads with a metal prong that was sunk into the shaft (figs. 12, 14, 15, 16, 17, 21, 25, 32, 33 and 37). 41. Finger-guard. After 1500, a type of guard with three fingerholes was introduced.

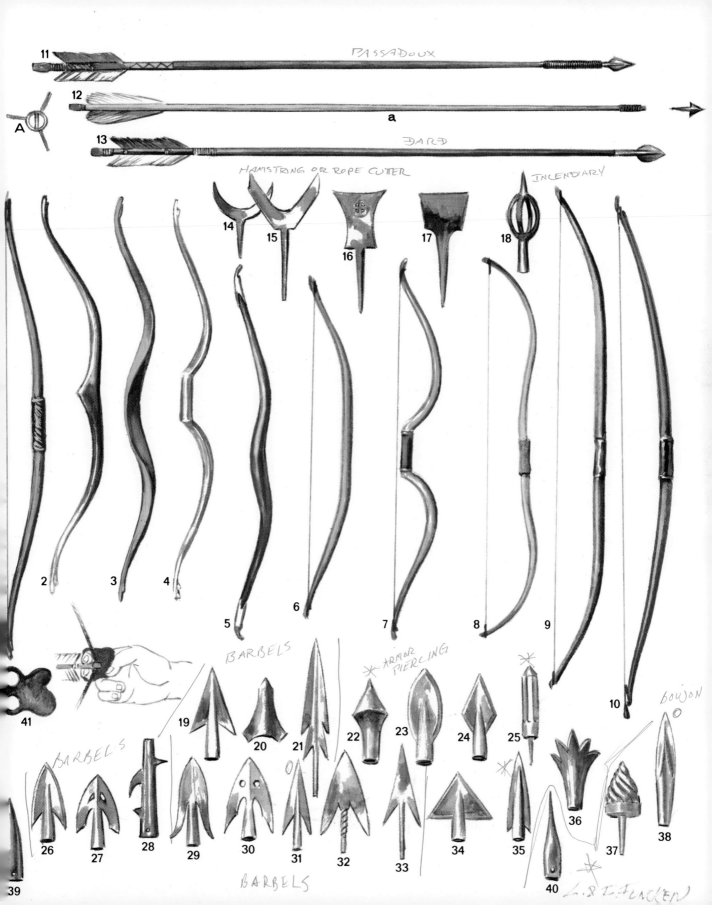

The hitting-power of the arrow is likewise generally under-estimated, as is its power of penetration. The tales of the chroniclers used to appear wildly fantastic – in particular those by Gérald de Galles, who recounts the mishap that befell a knight when he was pinned to his horse by a single arrow that pierced both his thighs.

Experiments carried out by modern experts have demonstrated that an arrow flighted with goose feathers, 90 centimetres long and weighing 700 to 800 grams, can pierce an oak plank 9 centimetres thick at close range and go through a plank of the same wood, two and a half centimetres thick, at a distance of 200 metres.

No coat of ring mail was able to stop an arrow fired at closer range than this, and armour of metal plates could be pierced up to a range of 100 metres. However, the most conclusive proof of the astonishing effectiveness of the bow and arrow is contained in the numerous references to cuirasses described as 'parve' or 'demi-parve' – that is, proof or semi-proof against projectiles, depending on their quality.

The reader will have a clearer picture from this of how impressive the volley of the 6,000 archers at Crécy was when it was repeated every twelve seconds, making five times 6,000 arrows – 30,000 in all – fired in sixty seconds. Every bowman carried two dozen arrows in his quiver, and so could say 'I have twenty-four Scotsmen under my belt'. Edward III's corps of archers could fire 144,000 arrows in four minutes – enough to stop the most resolute opponent in his tracks.

Effectiveness on this scale gave rise to the formation of a corps of French archers. The shortage of trained men meant that soldiers had to be hired. These were chiefly Italians, known as 'mercenaries', and were greatly inferior to the bowmen of England, Burgundy, and Brabant.

After the débâcle of Poitiers, free companies of archers were set up; the nobility, however, lost no time in having them disbanded, as they frowned upon these soldiers who had been recruited from the lower classes. As Juvenal des Ursins explains, with complete frankness, 'In a short time the French archers were so well trained in the use of the bow that they

THE BOW (iv)
1. French (15th century). 2. German (14th century). The same style of hat was also made in iron. 3. French bow (mid-15th century). 4. German bow (early 14th century). 5. English bow (early 15th century). 6. and 7. French bows (mid-15th century). 8. French bow (late 15th century). By this time archers were regarded merely as light, second-rank troops, and had been displaced by artillerymen and their firearms. The white cross that is shown in figs. 3 and 8 had been a characteristic feature of the uniform of the French soldier since the beginning of the 14th century, when King Edward III of England had made his troops who were sent to fight on the continent wear a uniform of a white tunic with a red cross on it. At the same period the Scots adopted the white cross of Saint Andrew as their emblem. These crosses, which started out by being very large, gradually shrank to the size of the one shown in fig. 5. 9. and 10. Free archers of Charles VII of France (mid-15th century). The sallets they are wearing as protective headgear had either a movable (fig. 10) or a fixed (fig. 9) visor. In the latter case, the sallet could be thrown back to leave the face free.

could outshoot the English; indeed, had they been united they would have been more powerful than the princes and nobles, and so the king was called upon to put an end to their activities.'

Thanks to the bow, however, the decline of heavy cavalry was already under way. The invention of firearms, and the rapid spread of their use among the common people, were to sound the death knell for the proud ideals of chivalry.

The bow continued to be used by the English army until 1595, when a special order of council banned the use of the weapon for military purposes for good.

The crossbow

THE CROSSBOW (i)
1. Primitive form of crossbow, ready for firing: a) bow; b) straps; c) stirrup; d) swivelling nut; e) stock; f) release trigger; g) pin or peg. 2. Rope method of cocking bowstring: a) pin; b) pulley; c) bowstring; d) nut. 3. Double hook. 4. Single hook. 5. Anglo-Norman crossbowman (12th century): a) pin; b) pulley; c) bowstring. The stave of the bow may have been made of ibex horn. 6. 'Belt and claw' method of bending bow (early 13th century). 7. Back view of 'belt and claw' method (mid-13th century). There is a fire arrow lying on the ground beside the bowman. 8. Crossbowman with his full set of equipment (late 14th century). 9. and 10. Bolts or quarrels. 11. Quivers.

The crossbow, or arbalest, whose name is derived from the Latin *arcubalista* (from *arcus* meaning 'bow', and *balista*, meaning 'ballista'), was used as a weapon in war from the mid-10th century onwards. William the Conqueror probably took crossbowmen with him to fight alongside his archers at Hastings in 1066.

At the beginning of the 12th century the troops of Louis the Fat of France included a contingent of crossbowmen; over a century later, in England, Edward I was still making extensive use of this type of soldier in his campaign against the Welsh in 1265. Princess Anna Comnena, the author of the *Alexiade*, described the use of this weapon in her highly stylized writings, while William of Tyre, who died around 1190, about forty years after her, also mentioned the crossbow in his *History of the Crusades* – a work, incidentally, of unusual sincerity and objectivity.

The crossbow was anathematized by the second Lateran Council in 1139, which described it as an 'instrument deathly and hateful to God' – *artem mortiferam et Deo odibilem*. An exception was made, however, in the case of its use against

2
a
b

3

4

5

6

1
a
b
c
d
e
f
g

7

8

9

10

11

L & F.
FONCKEN

heretics. The real intention behind this prohibition, which was repeated in a Papal brief issued by Innocent III, was to take a formidable weapon out of the hands of the common people. Richard the Lionheart[1] and Philip Augustus took no notice of these warnings and employed large numbers of crossbowmen.

This treacherous weapon, with which the most abject coward could ambush and kill the most fearless knight, was a constant feature of French armies, where it was used by both mounted troops and infantrymen. It even gave rise to a special title being created – 'Grand Master of the Crossbowmen' – which was first held by Thibaud de Montléart. Saint Louis of France awarded this coveted office to Mathieu de Beaume, and the last Grand Master, who died in 1534, was Aymar de Brie.[2] Charles IX, who ruled France from 1560 to 1574, finally banished the crossbow from the list of battle weapons with the following decree: 'Since bows and crossbows are not now used for defence, henceforth all crossbowmen and archers will be ordered to carry the arquebus instead of the bow or crossbow. . . .'

The development of the crossbow

The crossbow improved in performance as the material of the bow was gradually strengthened; this in turn made it necessary to devise increasingly powerful methods for cocking the bowstring. The bowpiece was first of all made out of yew, elm or maple; later materials to be used were whalebone, sinews or thin strips of wood and horn that had been carefully glued together. These were finally superseded by steel at the beginning of the 15th century.

THE CROSSBOW (ii)
1. Crossbow with windlass (also called a block and pulley crossbow): a) pins; b) some crossbows were fitted with a flexible strip of horn which fastened over the projectile and held it in place until the moment of firing. 2. Detail of the system of pulleys for the windlass. 3. French crossbowman of the late 14th century. 4. Genoese crossbowman with his pavise, which has the characteristic shape of an elongated heart. This shielded him while he turned his back to string his bow. The soldier was then said to be 'pavised'. 5. English crossbowman (15th century). This view shows the rope handles by which the pavise was held in place on the bowman's back. 6. Crossbowman stringing his weapon. Here the windlass is very rudimentary in form and has no pulleys (15th century). The reader will note the shape of the stock of the crossbows in figs. 3–5, which is similar to the butt of modern rifles used in target-shooting. As in the case of the rifle, this type of stock meant the bowman could take a long time over aiming without his left arm getting tired, because of its position close in to the body.

[1] Richard I was to be killed by a bolt from a crossbow at the siege of the castle of Chaluz, near Limoges in France, in 1199.
[2] In 1515 the office was combined with that of the Grand Master of Artillery; this followed immediately after the supreme rank of High Constable.

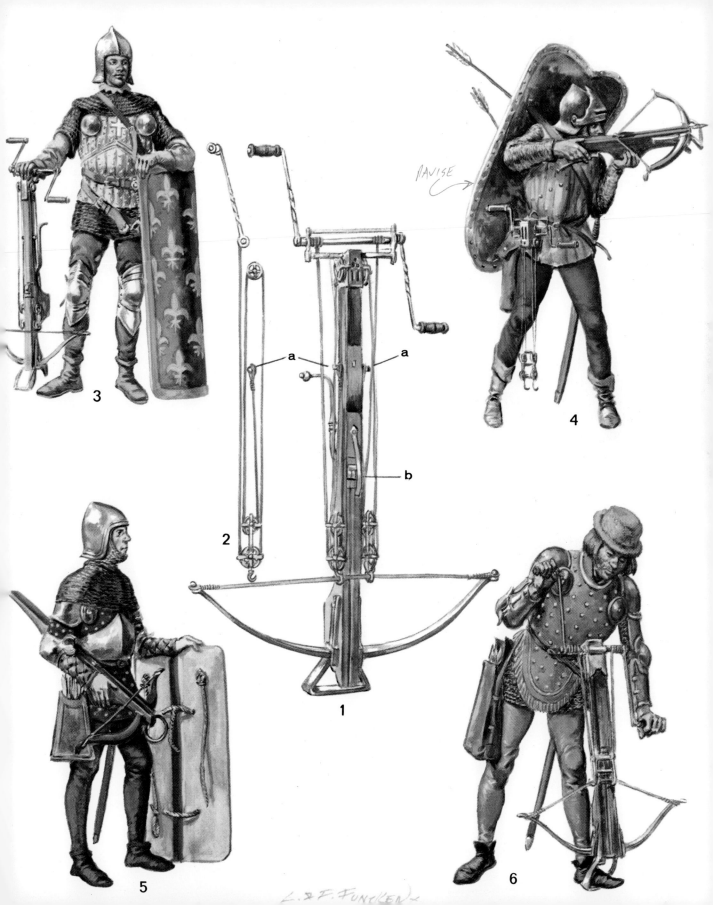

3

PAVISE

4

2

a   a

b

1

5

6

L. & F. FUNCKEN

Strengths and defects of the crossbow

The crossbow had the immense advantage of requiring neither a long period of training nor a marked degree of physical strength to wield it successfully. As a weapon it was best suited to siege warfare, where the crossbowmen could take his time in choosing his target, then aim his shot without tiring himself at all. The archer, on the other hand, had to 'pull' no less than a hundredweight (50 kilos) – a physical effort it is impossible to imagine anyone sustaining for more than a few seconds.

When fired straight ahead the bolt of the crossbow could pierce most cuirasses at a range of 65 to 90 yards (60 to 100 metres), depending on the power of the weapon.

In contrast the weight of the crossbow, and its low rate of firing (a maximum of two bolts per minute), were a handicap when fighting in open country. It has been calculated that at the battle of Crécy each Genoese crossbowman in the service of the king of France had to carry a weight of 90lbs (40 kilos) in all, taking into account his weapons, equipment and pavise. We can understand more readily why these crossbowmen were so wretchedly ineffective during this disastrous encounter when we think of the state they must have been reduced to after marching for 18 miles (30 kilometres) beforehand.

Pavises and mantlets

The illustrations show various types of large shields which were known as pavises. An essential part of the crossbowman's equipment, these shields, which weighed surprisingly little, were built over a framework of light wooden slats that had been skilfully glued together. Each side of the pavise was covered with horse or ass hide or buckskin, which was carefully stuck down with a very strong glue called 'maroufle', and then waterproofed with a layer of paint or varnish.

THE CROSSBOW (iii)

1. Hind's foot crossbow. This weapon, which was remarkably similar to the jack crossbow shown on the following page, was easy to recognize because of the position of the pins (a) which were located nearer to the nut (b). This, in fact, is the most reliable method of identifying these two types of crossbow, which in many cases have come down to us minus their jack or their hind's foot. A spring ring (c) has now replaced the stirrup, which was not necessary for such a short weapon. 2. and 3. Procedure for stringing a hind's foot bow (also called a goat's foot or bitch's foot): a) pins; b) nut. 4. Simplified form of hind's foot bow made of wood. 5. Crossbowman with a hind's-foot bow (15th century). 6. Crossbowman sheltering behind his pavise (c.1400). 7–22. Crossbow quarrels. Figs. 13, 20 and 21 are viretons (from the French *virer*, to turn) which had spiral feathering. The pot-bellied model shown in fig. 13, sometimes called a dondaine, had in some instances a feathering of brass vanes. Fig. 20 is an example of the 'demi-dondaine' type of crossbow. The refrain 'lafaridondon, lafaridondaine', once well known all over France, comes from the soldier's song which went 'à fĕri dondaine' (the dondaine has hit its mark).

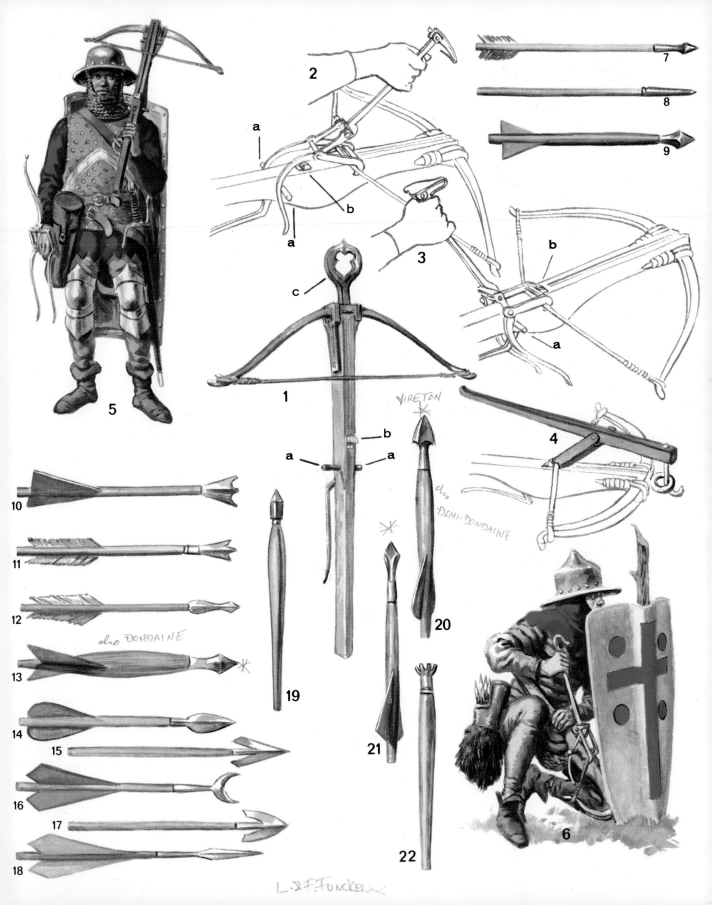

2

a

b

a

3

c

1

b

a   a

b

a

4

7

8

9

5

VIRETON

10

11

12

13   also DONDAINE

14

15

16

17

18

19

DEMI-DONDAINE

20

21

22

6

L.&F.FUNCKEN

In spite of its relative fragility, the pavise was, in fact, an excellent means of protection. When it was struck by an enemy arrow it gave under the impact, and was therefore far harder to penetrate than a conventional shield designed for hand-to-hand fighting.

The big heavy mantlets, on the other hand, were made out of very thick wood or iron, and were used during long sieges.

THE CROSSBOW (iv)

1. Jack crossbow: a) crank-handle; b) pinion box; c) claw; d) rack; e) strap; f) pin. Both the jack and the hind's foot model of crossbow are almost always known as 'cranequins'. In fact from the 14th to the 16th century the term cranequin (from the Walloon *crenekin*, a crossbow) was used to mean any cavalry crossbow that was strung by means of a hind's foot or jack; both these methods were more managable than the pulley system of the giant crossbow, which could not be operated on horseback. 1a) Method of operating a jack crossbow: A. when the string of the bow is pulled back it makes (b) swivel and the catch (d) engages in the ratchet mechanism (c); fig. A^1. shows the nut engaged; B. when the release trigger (e) is pressed, the catch (d) disengages from the ratchet (c) and the string is released, thereby propelling the projectile forward; at the same time the nut (a) has returned to a neutral position, allowing the bow to be reloaded as in fig. A; fig. B^1) shows the released nut. 2. Cranequineer or crennequineer of the guard of Charles the Bold (1473). 3. Great siege pavise with a V-shaped cut out of it for ease of sighting (early 15th century). 4. Siege mantlet (15th century). 5. Mounted crossbowman from an ordinance company of Charles the Bold (1473).

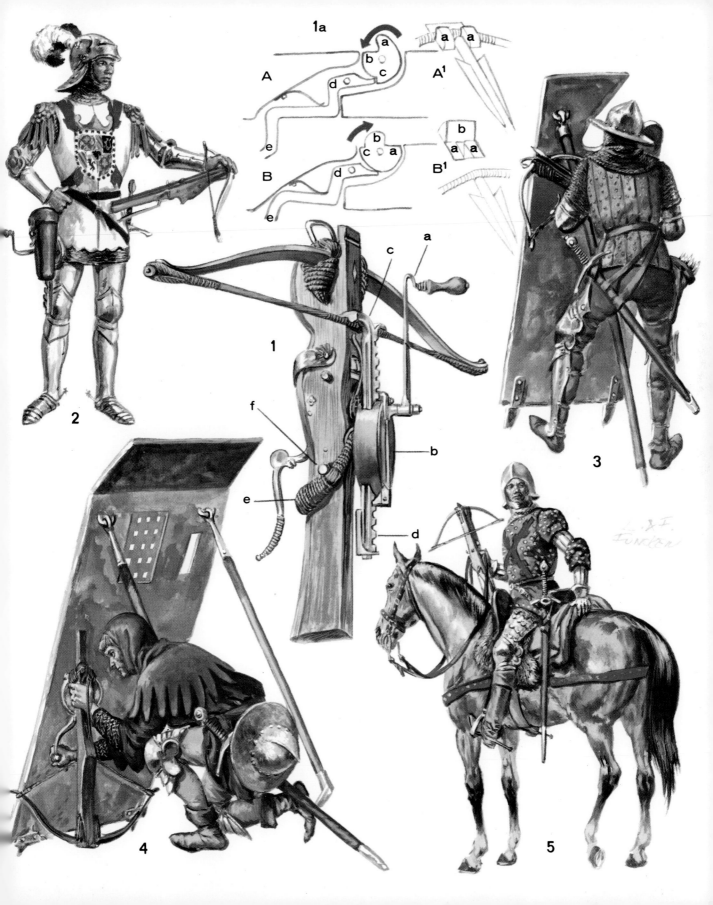

1a

A   A¹

B   B¹

1

2

3

4

5

Index

PLVS · ESP · EN · VOVS · HO

PLVS · E